CHICKE

THE LITTLE GUIDES

CHICKEN

FOG CITY PRESS

Published by Fog City Press
814 Montgomery Street
San Francisco, CA 94133 USA
Reprinted in 2000 (three times), 2001 (twice), 2002, 2003

Chief Executive Officer: John Owen
President: Terry Newell
Publisher: Lynn Humphries
Managing Editor: Janine Flew
Coordinating Designer: Helen Perks
Editorial Coordinator: Kiren Thandi
Production Manager: Caroline Webber
Production Coordinator: James Blackman
Sales Manager: Emily Jahn
Vice President International Sales: Stuart Laurence

Project Editor: Janine Flew
Designer: Lucy Bal

ISBN 1 875137 74 2

Color reproduction by Bright Arts Graphics (S) Pte Ltd
Printed by LeeFung-Asco Printers
Printed in China

A Weldon Owen Production

Contents

PART TWO

TECHNIQUES AND RECIPES

Introduction

A perfectly roasted chicken, crisp and golden, is more than just Sunday lunch. Simple and succulent, it represents home cooking at its best.

But roasting is only one way to make the most of the savory taste of chicken. Because this bird is such a superb carrier of other flavors, a wealth of memorable dishes has been created by talented cooks the world over to show it off. Coq-au-vin, a herb-and-wine simmered dish, is a favorite of the French country table. Latin cultures relish fajitas, tortilla-wrapped strips of grilled or sautéed chicken and peppers, while in India, chicken is

infused with an enticing depth of flavor from a coating of yogurt and curry spices.

Chicken is now more popular than ever. It is widely available, economical, and, because it is relatively low in fat and a good source of protein, increasingly appreciated for its contribution to a healthy diet. If you are looking for new ways to prepare this old favorite, try one of the dozens of recipes in this book. Behind each one are many years of kitchen experience and testing by culinary experts.

The Little Guide to *Chicken* also provides a wealth of practical information. Every important

Chicken with Duxelles Wrapped in Phyllo (see page 171).

technique—from cutting up a whole bird, to boning and skinning, to making stock and stuffing a bird, plus a thorough discussion of cooking methods— is demonstrated in vivid photographs and explained in easy-to-follow instructions.

An introductory chapter covers the basics of poultry handling, preparation and storage, while each succeeding chapter focuses on a particular cooking method. Each chapter builds on what you have already learned, with additional steps, special techniques and tempting recipes. The chapters are also color-coded, and every recipe features a "steps at a glance" box that uses these colors for quick reference to the photographic steps that illustrate its preparation. Valuable tips appear on virtually every page, from basic equipment requirements to helpful hints from the experts and stylish serving ideas. A glossary provides an overview of some of the ingredients used in the book.

U.S. cup measures are used throughout this book. Slight adjustments may need to be made to quantities if Imperial or Metric cups are used.

Whether you are a novice or an experienced cook, you will find a range of delicious recipes to tempt you, such as Spicy Spanish Kabobs, Honey-Glazed Drumsticks and Poussins with Cherry Sauce. The step-by-step sequences will explain the fine points in preparing such impressive fare as Roast Chicken with Pecan Rice Stuffing or Chicken Breasts with Tomato–Mint Pesto. To help you plan a menu, these and all the other recipes in the book are beautifully photographed along with suggested accompaniments.

PART ONE

THE BASICS

Cutting up a whole chicken is an easily learned skill that
allows you to get maximum value from the bird.
As a bonus, the trimmings make a flavorful stock to use
as a basis for soups, sauces and other dishes.

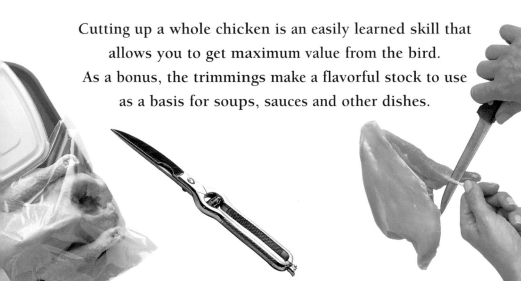

Cutting Up a Whole Chicken

Chicken is so versatile that almost every part is useful. Packaged, ready-to-cook chicken pieces are widely available and a great convenience, but cutting up a whole chicken yourself is not the daunting or time-consuming task that some view it to be. In fact, it is easily learned, quickly accomplished, and is such a basic technique for working with poultry that it should be part of every cook's repertoire, even if used only occasionally. Once you are comfortable handling a whole chicken, you are better able to put the parts to good use.

A further bonus is that when you are the butcher you not only produce portions that are custom-trimmed to suit your needs, you also save money. A whole chicken is usually less expensive to buy than an equivalent weight of poultry pieces because there are no labor costs built into the price.

This section will take you step by step through cutting up a whole bird. Another name for this technique is *disjointing* (jointing), because you cut through the elastic tendons and cartilage that surround the joint rather than through solid bone.

On the following pages you will also learn how to quickly and deftly bone breasts and legs, and how to remove the skin.

The Basics

Very little specialized equipment is needed to cut up a chicken other than a sharp, good-quality boning knife and poultry shears or kitchen scissors. Boning knives are typically 10 in/25 cm long, with thin, tapered, flexible blades that let you maneuver around the indentations of meat and bone. Poultry shears use a spring-lever action for more cutting power, although a pair of sturdy kitchen scissors will work almost as well in most cases. Work on a surface that is dishwasher safe, such as an acrylic cutting board. Avoid boards that are made of hard plastic; they will damage and dull your knives.

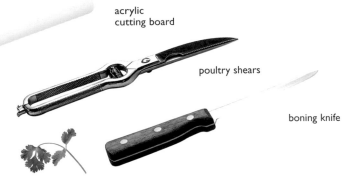

acrylic
cutting board

poultry shears

boning knife

Cutting through
a joint or cartilage
does less damage
to the knife
than cutting
through bone.

STEP 1

Cutting Off Legs

Pull the leg away from the body and slit the skin
between the thigh and body. Bend back the leg until
the thigh bone pops out of the hip joint. With the tip
of the knife, cut through the broken joint, meat and
skin to sever the leg (hold the knife against the backbone
as you cut). Repeat with the other leg.

To skin a
leg or thigh,
see pages 19
and 21.

STEP 2

Separating Legs

Place the leg skin-side up on the cutting board. To find
the joint, squeeze together the drumstick and thigh; the
flat, light-colored area at the top is the joint. Cut through
the joint to separate the drumstick and thigh into two
pieces. Repeat with the other leg.

Holding the wing away from the body lets you see where to cut.

STEP 3

Removing Wings

Pull the wing away from the body and slit the skin between the wing and body. Bend back the wing until the joint pops out. Cut through the broken joint, meat and skin to sever the wing. Repeat with the other wing.

It is easiest to cut through the white cartilage where the ribs meet on the side.

STEP 4

Separating Breast from Body

With poultry shears, kitchen scissors or a sharp boning knife, sever the ribs between the breast and back. Cut from the cavity end toward the neck end on both sides. Bend the breast and back halves apart, exposing the joints at the neck that connect the two halves. Cut through the joints.

You may have to cut gently around the breastbone to release it.

STEP 5

Removing Breastbone

With the breastbone facing you, use a small knife to slit open the membrane over the breastbone. Hold the breast at top and bottom and flex it up; the breastbone will pop out. Pull out the bone with your hand.

To skin chicken breasts, see page 19.

STEP 6

Cutting Breast in Half

Set the breast skin-side down. With a boning knife, cut down the center of the breast along the groove left by the breastbone. You will now have two half-breast portions.

As well as being delicious in its own right, chicken is also a superb carrier of other flavors. This makes it a versatile basis for a range of dishes, such as Tangy Marinated Fried Chicken (recipe on page 145).

Skinning and Boning Chicken

Removing the bones from chicken parts makes them cook faster; removing the skin allows the surface of the meat to brown. These steps prepare chicken for almost every cooking method used in this book: baking, broiling, grilling, barbecuing, sautéing, stir-frying and braising. When you can do these steps yourself, you not only save money, you have more flexibility. Familiarity with these techniques means that you can buy a whole chicken to cut up yourself as demonstrated on pages 14–16, then decide later whether to use the pieces with bones and/or skin intact or in a recipe that calls for boneless, skinless meat.

For breasts, deboning cuts away the breastbone and ribs. A boning knife is the best tool for this job, as its tapered, flexible blade slips easily between meat and bone. For thighs, which are smaller, use a boning knife or a small, sharp paring knife.

Stripping away skin is easily accomplished by hand, with the occasional assistance of a knife or kitchen scissors to release the skin from the meat.

Boned chicken breast halves provide neat servings ideally suited to grilling or sautéing. Boned chicken thighs give portions of dark meat that are best braised or quickly sautéed.

BASIC TOOLS FOR SKINNING AND BONING

For skinning and boning, use a boning knife and kitchen scissors, plus a work surface that can be easily cleaned, like a resilient acrylic board.

acrylic cutting board

boning knife

paring knife

kitchen scissors

STEPS FOR SKINNING AND BONING CHICKEN

If necessary, use a knife to cut the skin from the meat along the breastbone.

STEP I

Skinning Chicken Breasts or Thighs
Place a half breast skin-side up on a cutting board. Holding the piece with one hand, pull the skin away from the meat with the other hand, starting at the narrow end. Use the same technique for skinning chicken thighs.

19

Gently pull the bones away from the meat as you work, so you can see the cutting area.

STEP 2

Boning Chicken Breasts

Starting at one side of the ribs, cut the meat away from the bones with a boning knife. Continue cutting, pressing the flat side of the knife blade almost flat against the rib bones. Cut as close to the bone as possible.

Removing the tough tendon makes the meat more tender and easier to flatten or roll up.

STEP 3

Removing Tendon from Breast

To remove the tendon, pull it back with your fingers to stretch it out. With a knife, gently scrape the meat away from it until the entire length of the tendon is completely exposed. Sever and discard.

Lift the bone by the upper end as you cut around it.

STEP 4

Boning Chicken Thighs

Place the thigh on the cutting board with the meatier side down. With a boning knife or small, sharp knife, make a lengthwise slit through the meat to the bone. Carefully separate the meat from the bone by scraping it away around the bone and at the ends.

Cut the skin away at the foot end of the leg if it doesn't pull off completely.

The short side of the drumstick is on the inside of the leg.

STEP 5

Skinning Drumsticks or Legs

With a pair of sharp kitchen scissors, slit the skin from the joint end to the foot end on the shortest side of the drumstick. Remove the skin by holding onto the meaty end and pulling toward the foot end.

Storing Chicken

Careful handling of raw poultry helps prevent transmittal of food-borne illness. To keep fresh poultry safe to eat, it must be properly stored in the fridge or freezer until you need it. Leftover cooked chicken and accompaniments such as stuffing are equally susceptible to spoilage unless packaged and chilled as quickly as possible; never let them stand at room temperature for more than 2 hours.

Once purchased, store raw poultry in the coldest part of the refrigerator (not above 40°F/4°C) and use within 2 days. Cooked chicken, cut up or whole, should be used within 2 to 3 days. For longer storage, freeze a whole chicken for up to 1 year, chicken pieces for up to 9 months, and cooked chicken without sauce or liquid for up to 1 month. Never refrigerate or freeze a stuffed bird; always store stuffing separately. Frozen food keeps its quality at 0°F/minus 18°C or below, although some fridge-freezer compartments don't maintain this temperature. Check occasionally with a special freezer thermometer available in the housewares section of department stores, or from hardware shops.

The safest and best way to thaw frozen poultry is in the refrigerator. Allow 5 hours of thawing time per 1 lb/500 g.

Poultry that is packaged in freezer wrap can be thawed under cold water in the sink or a large bowl; change the water every half hour (a 3-lb/1.5-kg chicken will be ready to cook in about 12 hours). Defrosting at room temperature is not recommended as it creates a favorable environment for the growth of harmful organisms.

To avoid freezer burn—rough, dry areas where the meat has deteriorated from exposure to air—freeze poultry airtight and use within the suggested time limit. Specially constructed heavy-duty polyethylene freezer bags and ties are stocked on most supermarket shelves, as are coated freezer paper sheets. Reusable freezer-safe plastic containers are another practical alternative. Always date each package to keep track of when to use it, and note the contents.

STEPS FOR STORING CHICKEN

Let the water run over the outside and through the inside of the bird.

STEP 1

Rinsing Chicken

Before cooking or freezing, a whole bird or chicken pieces should be rinsed and dried. Rinse under cold running water. Let excess water run off, then pat the chicken dry inside and out with paper towels.

Seal tightly, pressing out as much air as possible.

STEP 2

Freezing Chicken

To freeze a whole chicken or chicken pieces, rinse and dry thoroughly, then place in a heavy-duty freezer bag, or wrap airtight in freezer paper. Label the contents, then date them.

Use a spoon or tongs, not fingers, for moving frozen meat from tray to storage container.

STEP 3

Freezing Cubed Chicken

Arrange leftover cooked cubed chicken on a tray in a single layer and freeze until firm. Transfer to freezer containers or freezer-safe bags; label and date.

When refrigerating or freezing leftovers, use heavy-duty containers or storage bags with a good seal.

STEP 4

Refrigerating Stuffing

After the meal, remove from the bird all stuffing and any remaining meat and store in separate containers. Never refrigerate or freeze stuffing in the bird.

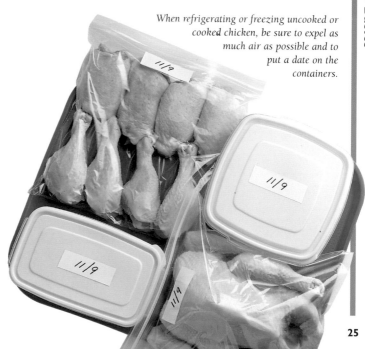

When refrigerating or freezing uncooked or cooked chicken, be sure to expel as much air as possible and to put a date on the containers.

About Stock

Stock is simply an infusion of a few basic ingredients—meat, water, vegetables and herbs. Its simplicity belies its versatility and the depth of flavor that it imparts. It forms the basis for many classic dishes, including paella, risotto, rich sauces and almost every kind of soup. Stocks made from uncooked meat are called white stocks; those made from roasted meats are known as brown stocks. Roasting the meat or vegetables for stocks intensifies the flavor of the stock by browning the exterior of the meat and caramelizing the natural sugars in the vegetables.

Meat and vegetable stocks need to be cooked for about 2 hours to extract the maximum flavor. Fish stock needs to be cooked for only about 30 minutes. The actual preparation time for all stocks is only about 20 minutes; once they are simmering, they need little attention apart from an occasional skimming to remove impurities.

Frozen, canned or concentrated stock or broth can be used if you don't have time to make your own stock. Purchased stock will have a fuller and fresher flavor if you simmer it briefly with aromatic vegetables such as onion, carrot, celery and leek.

Chicken Stock

One of the advantages of cutting up a whole chicken yourself
is putting the leftover bony pieces to use in homemade chicken stock.
Or purchase bones, necks and wings from your supermarket.

INGREDIENTS

3¹/₂ lb/1.75 kg bony chicken
pieces (bones, necks and wings
from 3 chickens)

3 stalks celery with leaves, cut up

2 carrots, cut up

1 large onion, cut up

2 sprigs parsley

1 teaspoon salt

¹/₂ teaspoon dried thyme, sage
or basil, crushed

¹/₄ teaspoon pepper

2 bay leaves

6 cups/48 fl oz/1.5 l cold water

Preparation time 20 minutes
Cooking time 2 hours
Makes about 5 cups/40 fl oz/
1.25 l stock and 2¹/₂ cups/15 oz/
425 g meat

STEPS AT A GLANCE	Page
■ Making chicken stock	28

METHOD FOR MAKING CHICKEN STOCK

In a large stockpot place chicken pieces, celery, carrots, onion, parsley, salt, thyme, sage or basil, pepper and bay leaves. Add water. Bring to boiling; reduce heat. Cover and simmer for 2 hours. Remove chicken.

To strain, pour stock through a large colander lined with 2 layers of pure cotton cheesecloth. Discard vegetables and seasonings. If using the stock while hot, skim off the fat. (Or chill the stock and lift off the fat.)

If desired, when cool enough to handle, remove meat from bones to reserve for another use. Discard bones. Store stock and reserved meat, in separate containers, in the fridge for up to 3 days or in the freezer for up to 6 months.

STEPS FOR MAKING CHICKEN STOCK

Lining the colander or sieve with cheesecloth helps trap fat, scum and particles that make stock cloudy and impair its flavor.

STEP I

Straining Stock

When the stock is done, remove from heat and lift out the chicken pieces with a slotted spoon or tongs. Pour stock through a large colander lined with 2 layers of 100 percent cotton cheesecloth into a large bowl. Cool the chicken pieces and remove the meat from the bones, if desired.

The Basics

If you need to use the stock right away while it is still hot, blot up the liquid fat from its surface with a folded paper towel.

STEP 2

Removing Fat

Let the stock cool briefly, then refrigerate it for at least several hours or overnight. With a large spoon or wire skimmer, skim off and discard the fat that has hardened into a layer on the surface of the stock.

Chicken stock will keep, covered, in the refrigerator for up to 3 days. Frozen stock can be kept for up to 6 months.

STEP 3

Freezing Stock

After the fat has been removed, transfer 1-cup/ 8-fl oz / 250-ml portions of stock to freezer-safe, heavy-duty plastic bags. Seal and date the bags, then lay them on their sides on a tray; freeze, remove from tray, and stack in the freezer until needed. Or, freeze small portions of stock in ice-cube trays, release the cubes, and store in labeled, dated bags.

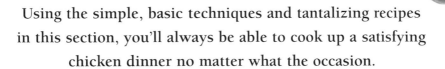

PART TWO

TECHNIQUES AND RECIPES

Using the simple, basic techniques and tantalizing recipes in this section, you'll always be able to cook up a satisfying chicken dinner no matter what the occasion.

ROASTING AND BAKING

Roasting Chicken

Who can resist a crisp, juicy roasted bird? As it cooks, it releases a wonderful aroma and a symphony of sizzles and crackles. The following recipe for Basic Roast Chicken is one that you will serve with pleasure again and again.

Rinse and dry the bird (see page 23, step 1), then secure the legs and wings as shown on page 37. Season the skin and set the bird on a rack in a roasting pan. To allow the underside to brown, it's best to elevate the bird on a rack so that it sits above the drippings.

The key to a perfectly roasted chicken is to cook it long enough so that it reaches a safe internal temperature (180°F/82°C in the thigh) yet is still moist and tender. This takes about 20 minutes for each pound/500 g of meat. Although a meat thermometer is the most accurate indicator of doneness, you can also judge it by jiggling the drumstick in its socket (it should move easily) and by piercing the thigh with a fork to check if the juices run clear and that there is no sign of pink in the meat (see tips on page 39).

paper towels and
acrylic cutting board

shallow roasting pan

You'll need kitchen string,
scissors, a brush, bowls and
a cutting board for preparation;
a roasting pan, a rack and a
bulb baster for cooking; and
paper towels and a thermometer
to check doneness when
roasting chicken.

bulb
baster

two small glass bowls

string

regular meat
thermometer

instant-read thermometer

soft brush

kitchen scissors

Basic Roast Chicken

This simple, delicious recipe can be varied endlessly. Experiment by rubbing the skin with your favorite herbs or spices, or by filling the cavity with different stuffings or even just a few fragrant cloves of garlic.

INGREDIENTS

3 to 3½ lb/1.5 to 1.75 kg whole broiler-fryer (roasting) chicken

Cooking oil or melted margarine or melted butter

1½ tablespoons mixed dried herbs, such as sage, thyme, oregano and/or rosemary

Preparation time 10 minutes
Cooking time 1¼ to 1½ hours
Makes 6 servings

METHOD FOR MAKING BASIC ROAST CHICKEN

Rinse chicken, then pat dry. Tie legs to tail; skewer neck skin to back; twist wings under the back. Brush bird with oil, margarine or butter and season with herbs.

Place bird, breast-side up, on a rack in a roasting pan.

Roast in a preheated 375°F/190°C/Gas Mark 4 oven for 1¼ to 1½ hours, or until juices run clear and the drumsticks move easily in their sockets. While the bird is cooking, spoon the drippings over it occasionally.

Cover loosely with foil, then let stand for 15 minutes before carving and serving.

Use heavy-gauge string that won't burn at roasting temperatures. Make sure it is made of a natural fiber; synthetic string will melt.

STEP 1

Tying Drumsticks to Tail

Lay the bird, breast-side up, on the cutting board. Cut off a 12-in/30-cm length of kitchen string. Overlap the legs, then loop the string around the ends and the tail; pull tight to secure. Tie in a bow (the string will be cut away before the bird is carved and served).

The wing tips will form a platform for the bird to sit on.

STEP 2

Twisting Wings Under

Fasten the neck skin to the back with metal skewers or toothpicks. Pull the wings out, twist the tips under the bird and push the wings in against the body.

For flavor, sprinkle with salt and pepper and other favorite seasonings.

STEP 3

Rubbing with Seasonings

Brush the entire bird with butter or oil as directed in the recipe. With your fingers, rub the seasonings onto the skin, then pat them to make them adhere.

A baster with a metal tube is preferable to one with a plastic tube, which could melt from the heat of the pan.

STEP 4

Basting the Bird

To add flavor and moisture, and to encourage browning, use a bulb baster or large spoon to baste the chicken occasionally with pan juices as it roasts. Do this quickly, as the oven temperature drops each time the door is opened.

DONENESS TESTS

TIP 1

Jiggling the Drumstick
To test for doneness, grasp the end of the drumstick with a paper towel. When it can be moved up and down and twisted easily in its socket, the chicken is done.

Be sure that the meat thermometer doesn't touch bone or the reading will be too high.

TIP 2

Using a Thermometer
Insert an instant-read meat thermometer into the center of the inside thigh muscle (do not touch bone). The temperature should be 180°F/82°C. (Or a regular meat thermometer can be inserted into the bird before roasting; it stays in the bird until it's done.)

Carving Chicken

Once the roast chicken is done, let it sit, loosely covered with aluminum foil to retain heat, for about 15 minutes before carving. During this resting period the internal juices drawn to the surface recirculate throughout the bird and the flesh firms up. If the chicken is carved too soon, these juices will pour out onto the board, and the meat will be dry rather than moist and will shred when cut instead of slicing neatly.

Transfer the chicken to a grooved carving board and remove any stuffing to a serving dish. To carve, follow the basic steps shown on pages 41–43.

Despite the mystique that surrounds it, carving is simple once you know where to cut— and if you use the proper tools. A sharp carving knife and large, two-pronged fork are essential. Select a knife with a long, flexible blade made of a material that will take and maintain a sharp edge. If the blade is dull, it will hack apart even the most beautifully prepared bird and ruin its appearance. A dull knife also is more likely to slip and cut you. Use the fork to hold the bird steady as you work. If you're not confident using a traditional carving knife, you may find an electric knife easier to work with.

BASIC TOOLS FOR CARVING CHICKEN

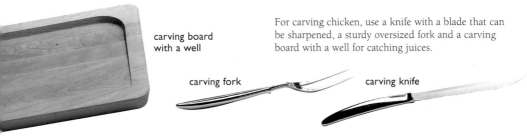

carving board with a well

For carving chicken, use a knife with a blade that can be sharpened, a sturdy oversized fork and a carving board with a well for catching juices.

carving fork

carving knife

STEPS FOR CARVING CHICKEN

Use a carving board that is big enough to hold the bird plus some of the carved pieces.

To find the joint, pull the leg all the way down until the thigh joint pops out.

STEP 1

Cutting Legs from Roast Chicken
Set the fork in the center of the chicken to keep it stable. Pull one leg away from the body and cut through the skin between the thigh and body with a sharp knife. Repeat on the other side.

STEP 2

Cutting Legs in Half

Place the leg, skin-side up, on the carving board. Cut through the joint between the drumstick and thigh to separate the leg into two pieces. Repeat with the other leg.

Rather than cutting off each breast half in a single piece, you can carve away the meat in several slices directly from the bird, slicing parallel to the ribs.

STEP 3

Removing Breast Meat

To remove a breast half in one whole piece, cut along one side of the breastbone and guide the knife down the rib bones, much as you would bone an uncooked breast (see page 20). Repeat with the second breast half.

If desired, remove the skin before slicing.

STEP 4

Slicing Breast Meat

Once the breast halves are removed from the body, slice each into pieces of an even thickness. If you cut across the grain of the meat, the slices will be more attractive.

STEP 5

Removing Wings

As a final step, separate the wings from the body by cutting through the joints where the wing bones and backbone meet, similar to removing the wings on an uncooked bird (see page 15).

Baking Boneless Chicken Breasts

The mild, juicy goodness of boned, skinned chicken breasts makes them the perfect starting point for a delicious baked main course. When pounded into rectangles of an even thickness, they are an ideal base for tempting fillings such as the seasoned caper and cream cheese mixture used on these pages (the recipe is on pages 80–81).

Rolled up and baked, then sliced and served with a tasty sauce, boneless breasts are succulent party fare. This cut of meat is so highly regarded that its classic culinary name is *suprême*.

The best suprêmes are the ones you have trimmed yourself. Steps for skinning and boning chicken breasts are on pages 19–21. Or you can have the butcher prepare them for you. Breasts to be filled will roll up more easily and cook more uniformly if they are first pounded with a metal meat mallet to square off their shape.

BASIC TOOLS FOR BAKING BONELESS CHICKEN BREASTS

You'll need these basic tools to flatten, fill and bake a stuffed boneless breast. A boning knife is used to bone the breasts.

small bowl

spreading knife

baking dish

meat mallet

boning knife

plastic wrap and acrylic cutting board

slicing knife

Roasting and Baking

You can also place the chicken in a heavy-duty plastic bag and pound it.

Store the flattened chicken in the plastic wrap until you are ready to use it.

STEP 1

Pounding Chicken Breasts

Place each chicken breast half, boned-side up, between 2 pieces of plastic wrap. Working from the center to the edges, pound with the flat side of a mallet to the desired thickness (a 1/8-in/3-mm-thick rectangle for stuffing).

Leave enough bare space around the edges so the meat can be folded over the filling.

STEP 2

Placing Filling on Breasts

Set the pounded breast halves on the work surface, skinned-side down. With a small spatula or spoon, spread an even layer of filling on each piece.

If the filling is not cheese, butter or anything that melts, the sides don't need to be tucked in. Secure the rolls with toothpicks, if necessary, but remember to remove them before slicing and serving.

STEP 3

Rolling Up Breasts

Fold the ends over the filling, then roll up like a jelly roll, starting from a long side. Brown the rolls by sautéeing them in a little butter or oil, then transfer them to a baking dish and bake until tender and fully cooked.

Another way to test for doneness is to see if the meat juices run clear when the rolls are pricked with a fork or skewer.

STEP 4

Testing for Doneness

After the stuffed rolls have cooked, remove the baking dish from the oven onto a rack or trivet. Slice into one of the rolls. If no pink remains, the chicken is done. Set the rolls on a board and slice them.

Roast Chicken with Pecan Rice Stuffing

**If you can't find wild pecan rice
(a regional grain from Louisiana), use long-grain rice instead
and add pecans to the stuffing to give it a similarly nutty flavor.**

INGREDIENTS

One 7-oz package wild pecan rice or 1 cup/7 oz/200 g long-grain rice

Chicken stock

1/2 cup/2 1/2 oz/75 g chopped fresh fennel bulb

1/4 cup/3/4 oz/20 g chopped green (spring) onion

1 tablespoon margarine or butter

1/2 cup/2 oz/60 g pecans (optional)

1/3 cup/1 1/2 oz/45 g dried cranberries, dried tart red cherries or dried currants

1/4 cup/1/2 oz/15 g snipped fresh parsley

3 to 3 1/2 lb/1.5 to 1.75 kg whole broiler-fryer (roasting) chicken

1 tablespoon cooking oil, or margarine or butter, melted

For a spectacular presentation, place a whole roast chicken on a large platter and garnish it with fresh herbs, orange slices and grapes. Carve at the table and serve extra stuffing alongside.

Preparation time 30 minutes
Roasting time 1¼ to 1½ hours
Makes 6 servings

STEPS AT A GLANCE	Page
▪ Stuffing chicken	51
▪ Roasting chicken	37–38
▪ Carving chicken	41–43

Prepare pecan rice according to directions on the package, except use chicken stock in place of water and omit salt. Or, bring 2 cups of stock to boiling, add the long-grain rice and simmer, covered, for about 20 minutes, or until rice is tender and all the liquid is absorbed. Set aside.

Meanwhile, in a medium frying pan cook the fennel bulb and green (spring) onion in 1 tablespoon butter or margarine until tender. Stir in pecans (if using), cranberries, cherries or currants and parsley; heat through. Stir into the cooked rice.

Rinse chicken; pat dry. Spoon some of the stuffing loosely into the neck cavity; skewer neck skin to back. Lightly spoon stuffing into the body cavity. (Put any remaining stuffing into a 2 pt/1 qt/1 l casserole. Bake the stuffing in the casserole, covered, for 30 to 35 minutes while the chicken is cooking.)

Tie the drumsticks securely to the tail. Twist the wing tips under the back. Place the chicken, breast-side up, on a rack in a shallow roasting pan. Brush the chicken with cooking oil, margarine or butter.

Roast, uncovered, in a preheated 375°F/190°C/Gas Mark 4 oven for 1¼ to 1½ hours, or until the juices run clear and the drumsticks move easily in their sockets. Cover loosely with aluminum foil and let stand for about 15 minutes before carving.

STEPS FOR STUFFING CHICKEN

If you don't like traditional stuffing, a simple and flavorful alternative is to put a few sprigs of fresh herbs, half a lemon or several cloves of garlic into the cavity.

STEP 1

Skewering Neck

Loosely fill the neck cavity with prepared rice stuffing. Close off by pulling the neck skin over the opening and securing it to the back with a small metal skewer.

STEP 2

Stuffing Body

Spoon the stuffing into the body cavity. Fill the cavity, but don't pack it with stuffing, as the mixture will expand during roasting. When the drumsticks are tied together, they will cover the exposed stuffing.

Chicken with Lemon Stuffing

**Fresh lemon juice and herbs invigorate the flavor of the
stuffing in this simple roast chicken.**

INGREDIENTS

STUFFING

7 cups/14 oz/440 g dry
bread cubes

1/2 cup/2 1/2 oz/75 g finely
chopped onion

2 teaspoons finely shredded
lemon peel

1/2 teaspoon dried marjoram,
crushed

1/2 teaspoon dried thyme,
crushed

1/4 teaspoon salt

1/4 teaspoon pepper

1 clove garlic, minced

1 lightly beaten egg

1/2 cup/4 oz/125 g butter or
margarine, melted

3 tablespoons water

2 tablespoons lemon juice

ROAST CHICKEN

3 to 3 1/2 lb/1.5 to 1.75 kg whole
broiler-fryer (roasting) chicken

1 tablespoon cooking oil, or
butter or margarine, melted

PAN GRAVY

1/4 cup/2 fl oz/60 ml reserved fat
skimmed from pan drippings

Skimmed pan drippings

1/4 cup/1 oz/30 g all-purpose
(plain) flour

Chicken stock or water

1/2 teaspoon finely shredded
lemon peel

Salt

Pepper

Tender, juicy slices of roast chicken, steamed asparagus and carrots make an appealing dinner anytime. Pan gravy is spooned over each portion.

Preparation time 35 minutes
Roasting time 1¼ to 1½ hours
Makes 6 servings

STEPS AT A GLANCE	Page
■ Stuffing chicken	51
■ Roasting chicken	37–38
■ Carving chicken	41–43
■ Making gravy	55

For stuffing, in a mixing bowl stir together the bread cubes, onion, lemon peel, marjoram, thyme, salt, pepper and garlic. In another bowl stir together the egg, melted butter or margarine, water and lemon juice. Add to the bread cubes; toss to mix.

For roast chicken, rinse the chicken and pat it dry. Spoon some of the stuffing loosely into the neck cavity; skewer neck skin to back. Lightly spoon stuffing into the body cavity. (Put any remaining stuffing into a 2 pt/ 1 qt/1 l casserole. Drizzle with 1 to 2 tablespoons of extra water or stock. Bake, covered, for 20 to 30 minutes with the chicken.)

Tie the drumsticks securely to tail. Twist the wing tips under the back. Place the chicken, breast-side up, on a rack in a shallow roasting pan. Brush the chicken with oil, butter or margarine.

Roast, uncovered, in a preheated 375°F/190°C/Gas Mark 4 oven for 1¼ to 1½ hours, or until juices run clear and drumsticks move easily in their sockets.

Cover with foil and let stand for 15 minutes before carving.

For pan gravy, pour the pan drippings from the roast chicken into a large measuring cup. Also scrape the browned bits from the bottom of the pan into the cup. Skim and reserve fat from drippings. Return ¼ cup/ 2 fl oz/60 ml of the fat to the roasting pan (discard remaining fat). Stir in flour and cook until bubbly. Add enough stock or water to remaining drippings in the measuring cup to equal 2 cups/16 fl oz/500 ml. Add all at once to flour mixture. Cook and stir over medium heat until thickened and bubbly. Add lemon peel. Season to taste with salt and pepper.

A gravy separator, available from kitchen supply shops, makes easy work of separating the cooking fat from the rest of the pan drippings.

STEP 1

Cooking Flour

Pour 1/4 cup/2 fl oz/60 ml reserved fat, skimmed from the drippings, into the roasting pan. Sprinkle the flour over the fat while stirring; cook until bubbly.

Add the browned bits from the bottom of the pan to the gravy; they will give it extra flavor.

STEP 2

Thickening Gravy

Add enough stock or water to the remaining pan drippings to make 2 cups/16 fl oz/500 ml liquid, then pour into the flour mixture. Cook over medium heat, stirring constantly, until thickened.

Seasoned under the skin, then roasted to crispy perfection, this glorious bird looks dramatic on a platter garnished with fresh chili peppers and cilantro sprigs.

56

Roast Chicken
with Chili–Cilantro Butter

Because chili peppers contain volatile oils that can burn
skin and eyes, avoid direct contact with them as much as possible.
Cilantro (also called fresh coriander or Chinese parsley) is the
leafy part of the plant that also gives us coriander seed.

INGREDIENTS

4 cloves garlic, peeled

2 fresh red chili peppers,
stemmed, cored, seeded and
coarsely chopped

1/4 cup/2 oz/60 g butter or
margarine, cut into 4 pieces

1 cup cilantro (fresh coriander or
Chinese parsley)

3 to 3 1/2 lb/1.5 to 1.75 kg whole
broiler-fryer (roasting) chicken

Paprika

Onion salt

Preparation time 25 minutes
Roasting time 1¼ to 1½ hours
Makes 6 servings

STEPS AT A GLANCE	Page
■ Seasoning chicken under the skin	59
■ Roasting chicken	37–38
■ Carving chicken	41–43

In a food processor bowl or blender container finely chop the garlic cloves and red chilies. (Keep lid closed while processing and open lid cautiously, being careful not to inhale directly over the bowl.) Add butter or margarine and cilantro (coriander); process or blend until nearly smooth.

Beginning at the neck of the bird, loosen the skin from the breast by working your fingers and thumb toward the tail. Loosen as much skin as possible without piercing the skin. Turn the chicken over and continue to loosen skin down both sides of the backbone, thighs and legs. Spread the butter mixture,

1 tablespoon at a time, under the skin on the chicken breast and back. Rub your thumb on top of the skin to distribute the butter mixture under the skin as evenly as possible.

Tie legs to tail; pull neck skin to back and skewer. Twist wing tips under back. Sprinkle chicken with paprika and onion salt.

Place bird, breast-side up, on a rack in a shallow roasting pan. Roast, uncovered, in a preheated 375°F/190°C/Gas Mark 4 oven for 1¼ to 1½ hours, or until the juices run clear and the drumsticks move easily in their sockets. Cover loosely with foil and let stand for 15 minutes before carving.

STEPS FOR SEASONING CHICKEN UNDER THE SKIN

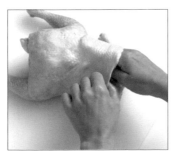

STEP 1

Loosening Skin

Beginning at the neck end of the bird, work your hand under the skin to loosen it. Start over the breast first, from the neck toward the tail. Then continue down both sides of the backbone to the thighs and legs. Be careful not to pierce the skin.

As well as adding flavor, seasoning with butter under the skin helps keep the meat tender and succulent.

STEP 2

Distributing Butter

Put 1 tablespoon of the butter mixture at a time under the skin at the breast and back. With a sliding motion, rub your thumb over the skin to distribute the butter as evenly as possible.

Roast Chicken with Minted Spice Rub

This combination of spices has a Middle Eastern flair
and forms a wonderfully flavorful, crunchy crust.
Sprinkle the cavity of the chicken with any leftover spices.

INGREDIENTS

3 to 3 1/2 lb/1.5 to 1.75 kg whole broiler-fryer (roasting) chicken

2 teaspoons dried mint leaves, crushed

1 teaspoon ground cardamom

1/2 teaspoon ground cinnamon

1/2 teaspoon salt

1/4 teaspoon pepper

1 tablespoon cooking oil or olive oil

Fresh mint leaves (optional)

Preparation time 15 minutes
Cooking time 1 1/4 to 1 1/2 hours
Makes 6 servings

Sautéed zucchini, and couscous mixed with peas and diced carrots, complement the earthy spices used on this roasted bird.

Rinse chicken; pat dry. In a small mixing bowl stir together the dried mint, cardamom, cinnamon, salt and pepper. Brush chicken with oil, then rub mint-spice mixture onto the skin. Skewer neck skin to back, tie legs to tail and twist wing tips under back.

Place bird, breast-side up, on a rack in a shallow roasting pan. Roast, uncovered, in a preheated 375°F/190°C/Gas Mark 4 oven for 1 1/4 to 1 1/2 hours, or until juices run clear and drumsticks move easily in their sockets. Cover loosely with foil, then let stand for 15 minutes before carving. If desired, garnish with fresh mint leaves.

About Cardamom

A member of the ginger family, cardamom is a tall perennial shrub that grows wild in the monsoon forests of southern India and Sri Lanka. Large-scale cultivation also takes place in these countries, as well as in Guatemala. The fruits, or cardamom pods, are small, green, oval capsules. Each contains 15 to 20 aromatic dark-brown seeds that have a pungent, spicy, lemony flavor and a eucalyptus-like scent.

Cardamom was first used by the ancient Egyptians and then by the ancient Greeks and Romans. It came to Europe along the old spice routes, and was not cultivated until 1800. It is an essential ingredient in Indian cookery, where it adds flavor to curries, coffee and cakes. In the Middle East it features in sweets and sweet pastries and in the strong coffee of the region to make the flavor more mellow. It is also used in the cakes, breads, pastries and mulled wines of Northern Europe. In the United States and France, the essential oil is used in perfumery.

Loose seeds and ground cardamom lose their flavor quickly, so it is best to buy whole pods and to remove and crush the seeds just before using them. Avoid brown cardamoms; these are not true cardamoms and have an unpleasant flavor. Cardamom combines well with fruit; use the seeds when baking apples or poaching pears, or add ground cardamom to fruit salads.

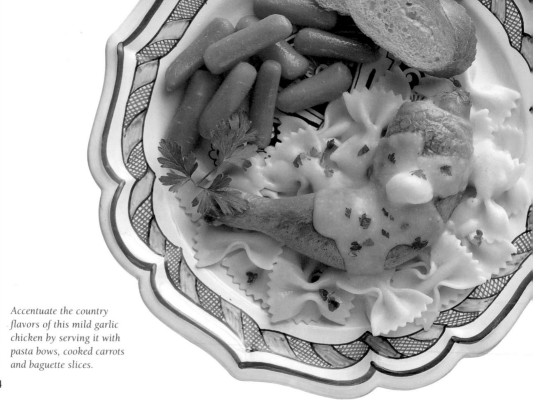

Accentuate the country flavors of this mild garlic chicken by serving it with pasta bows, cooked carrots and baguette slices.

Chicken with Roasted Garlic Sauce

While raw garlic is potent and sharp,
when oven-roasted it takes on a mellow, delicate sweetness.

INGREDIENTS

3 to 3½ lb/1.5 to 1.75 kg whole broiler-fryer (roasting) chicken

15 cloves garlic, peeled

1 tablespoon minced garlic (about 6 cloves)

1 teaspoon salt

1 tablespoon cooking oil

1 cup/8 fl oz/250 ml water

¼ cup/1 oz/30 g all-purpose (plain) flour

Chicken stock

1 tablespoon lemon juice

Pepper

Snipped fresh parsley (optional)

Preparation time 30 minutes
Cooking time 1¼ to 1½ hours
Makes 6 servings

Roasting and Baking

Rinse chicken; pat dry. Flatten 5 of the garlic cloves and place inside the body cavity of the chicken. Skewer neck skin to back; tie legs to tail. Twist wings under back. Combine the minced garlic and salt. Brush chicken with oil, then rub the garlic-salt mixture onto the skin.

Place chicken, breast-side up, on a rack in a shallow roasting pan. In another ovenproof pan combine the remaining garlic cloves and the water. Place both pans in a preheated 375°F/190°C/Gas Mark 4 oven and roast, uncovered, for 1¼ to 1½ hours, or until juices run clear and the drumsticks move easily in their sockets. Spoon drippings over chicken occasionally. If necessary, cover chicken with foil for the last 20 minutes of roasting to prevent overbrowning. Check garlic cloves to be sure they have enough water to cook gently, but not burn. Transfer chicken to a serving platter. Let stand, covered loosely with foil, for 15 minutes before carving.

Meanwhile, pour pan drippings into a large measuring cup. Also scrape any browned bits into the cup. Skim and reserve fat from the drippings. Place ¼ cup/2 fl oz/60 ml of the fat into a medium saucepan (discard remaining fat). Stir in flour; cook and stir for 2 minutes, or until flour is golden. To the remaining drippings in measuring cup, add the cooked garlic cloves and their cooking water and enough chicken stock to equal 2 cups/ 16 fl oz/500 ml. Add all at once to flour mixture. Cook and stir over medium heat until sauce is thickened and bubbly. Cook and stir for 2 minutes more. Stir in lemon juice and season to taste with pepper. If desired, garnish with parsley.

Poussins with Vegetable Stuffing

**If you can't find poussins, use widely available Cornish game hens
to make this country-style dish. If you prefer, roast 4 poussins
and serve a whole bird to each person.**

INGREDIENTS

1 cup/5 oz/155 g finely chopped carrots

1 cup/5 oz/155 g finely chopped celery

1/3 cup/1 1/2 oz/45 g finely chopped leek

1/2 cup/1 1/2 oz/45 g sliced fresh mushrooms

1/2 cup/2 1/2 oz/75 g finely chopped onion

2 tablespoons margarine or butter

1/2 teaspoon dried thyme, crushed

1/2 teaspoon salt

1/4 teaspoon pepper

1/4 cup/2 fl oz/60 ml heavy (double) cream (optional)

2 poussins or Cornish game hens, each 1 to 1 1/2 lb/ 500 to 750 g

1 tablespoon cooking oil

Preparation time 30 minutes
Cooking time 1¼ to 1½ hours
Makes 4 servings

In a large skillet (frying pan) cook carrots, celery, leek, mushrooms and onion in hot margarine or butter for about 5 minutes, or until vegetables are crisp-tender, but not brown. Add thyme, salt and pepper. If desired, stir in cream to moisten the mixture. Cool vegetable mixture slightly.

Rinse birds; pat dry. Spoon some of the vegetable mixture loosely into the body cavity of each bird. Pull neck skin, if present, to back of each bird. Twist wing tips under back. Tie legs to tail. Put any remaining stuffing into a small casserole; cover and chill. Place the birds, breast-sides up, on a rack in a shallow roasting pan. Brush birds with cooking oil. Cover loosely with foil.

Bake in a preheated 375°F/190°C/Gas Mark 4 oven for 20 minutes. Uncover birds. Bake 20 to 25 minutes more, or until juices run clear and the drumsticks move easily in their sockets. Add extra stuffing, covered, to oven during the last 20 minutes of roasting. Let birds stand, covered loosely with foil, for 15 minutes before serving. To serve, cut each bird in half. Serve with stuffing.

Bake a few quartered red potatoes in oil in the same oven as the poussins for an easy accompaniment.

The combination of fruit-based sauces
and game birds has variations in
cuisines around the world.
This rendition pairs
cherries with poussins
for a contemporary
effect.

Poussins with Cherry Sauce

Poussins are simple to prepare and make an impressive meal.
For an attractive presentation, surround the birds with whole sprigs of fresh
rosemary or thyme and sprinkle them with shredded orange peel.

INGREDIENTS

2 poussins or Cornish game hens, each 1 to 1 1/2 lb/ 500 to 750 g

2 teaspoons cooking oil

1/8 teaspoon salt

1/8 teaspoon pepper

3/4 cup/7 1/2 oz/240 g cherry jam

1 tablespoon cider vinegar

1 tablespoon frozen orange juice concentrate, thawed

1 tablespoon kirsch (optional)

1 tablespoon water

2 teaspoons cornstarch (cornflour)

Preparation time 20 minutes
Cooking time 1 to 1 1/2 hours
Makes 4 servings

STEPS AT A GLANCE	Page
■ Roasting chicken	37–38

Halve the birds and place cut-side down on a rack in a roasting pan. Brush birds with cooking oil; sprinkle with salt and pepper.

Bake, uncovered, in a preheated 375°F/190°C/Gas Mark 4 oven for 1 to 1½ hours, or until juices run clear.

Meanwhile, in a small saucepan melt the jam over low heat. Stir together the vinegar, orange juice concentrate, kirsch (if desired), water and cornstarch (cornflour). Add to saucepan. Cook and stir over medium heat until thickened and bubbly. Cook and stir for 2 minutes more. Serve sauce with birds.

Carolina-Style Oven-Barbecued Chicken

To approximate the slow-cooked, vinegary taste
of Carolina barbecue, roast chicken legs, then shred the meat
and mix it with a pungent sauce.

INGREDIENTS

1 teaspoon sugar

1 teaspoon garlic powder

1 teaspoon paprika

1/2 teaspoon ground allspice

1/2 teaspoon black pepper

1/4 teaspoon salt

1/4 teaspoon dry mustard powder

1/8 teaspoon ground red (cayenne) pepper

4 whole chicken legs, skinned (about 2 1/2 lb/1.25 kg)

2 tablespoons vinegar

2 tablespoons water

1 tablespoon honey

1 teaspoon Worcestershire sauce

1/2 to 1 teaspoon bottled hot chili pepper sauce

1/2 teaspoon prepared mustard

6 hamburger buns, split and toasted

METHOD FOR MAKING CAROLINA-STYLE OVEN-BARBECUED CHICKEN

Preparation time 25 minutes
Roasting time 45 minutes
Makes 6 servings

In a small mixing bowl combine sugar, garlic powder, paprika, allspice, black pepper, salt, dry mustard and ground red (cayenne) pepper. Rub spice mixture onto chicken legs.

Place chicken on a rack in a shallow roasting pan. Bake, uncovered, in a preheated 375°F/190°C/Gas Mark 4 oven for 45 minutes, or until chicken is tender and no longer pink.

Cool chicken slightly. Remove chicken meat from bones; shred meat.

In a medium saucepan combine vinegar, water, honey, Worcestershire sauce, hot chili pepper sauce and prepared mustard. Stir in shredded chicken; heat through. Serve in hamburger buns.

Try a scoop of coleslaw with these spicy filled buns. It's not only a terrific flavor combination, but the coleslaw will cool hot tongues as well.

Piled high on a festive platter, these baked chicken wings are impossible to resist.

Smoky Chicken Wings

Serve these pungent wings whole as a main course.
Or, to offer them as snacks or finger food, remove tips and cut wings
in half at the joint so they can be easily handled.
Liquid smoke (hickory oil) is available at gourmet grocers and delicatessens.

INGREDIENTS

1 cup/8 fl oz/250 ml water

1/3 cup/2 1/2 fl oz/80 ml liquid
smoke (hickory oil)

2 tablespoons Worcestershire
sauce

3 tablespoons dried parsley flakes

1 1/2 teaspoons dried oregano,
crushed

1 1/2 teaspoons paprika

3/4 teaspoon garlic powder

3/4 teaspoon salt

3/4 teaspoon pepper

16 chicken wings
(about 3 lb/1.5 kg)

Preparation time 15 minutes
Marinating time 1 hour
Baking time 30 to 35 minutes
Makes 4 servings

STEPS AT A GLANCE   Page

In a medium mixing bowl combine water, liquid smoke (hickory oil), Worcestershire sauce, parsley flakes, oregano, paprika, garlic powder, salt and pepper. Place chicken wings or pieces in a plastic bag set in a shallow dish. Pour marinade over chicken in bag. Seal bag and turn to coat chicken wings or pieces well.

Marinate in the refrigerator for about 1 hour, turning bag once. Remove chicken from bag; discard marinade. Place chicken wings or pieces on a foil-lined baking sheet or shallow baking pan. Bake in a preheated 400°F/200°C/Gas Mark 5 oven for 30 to 35 minutes, or until chicken is tender and no longer pink.

Stuffed Chicken Breasts with Red Pepper Coulis

The bell pepper coulis, or puréed sauce, makes a colorful background for chicken. A swirl of sour cream through the sauce will add another pretty touch to the dish.

INGREDIENTS

STUFFED CHICKEN BREASTS

3 oz/90 g packaged cream cheese, softened

2 tablespoons grated Parmesan cheese

1 tablespoon drained capers

1 tablespoon milk

1 clove garlic, minced

Dash pepper

4 boneless, skinless chicken breast halves (1 lb/500 g total)

1 tablespoon olive oil or cooking oil

1/4 cup/2 fl oz/60 ml dry white wine

RED PEPPER COULIS

2 medium-sized red bell peppers (capsicums), roasted and peeled, or 3/4 cup/5 oz/ 155 g bottled roasted bell peppers, drained

2 cloves garlic, minced

1 tablespoon olive oil or cooking oil

1/4 cup/2 fl oz/60 ml half-and-half (half cream) or light (single) cream

2 teaspoons anchovy paste

1 tablespoon drained capers

79

Preparation time 25 minutes
Baking time 20 to 25 minutes
Makes 4 servings

STEPS AT A GLANCE	Page
■ Skinning and boning chicken	19–21
■ Baking boneless chicken breasts	46–47

For stuffed chicken breasts, in a small mixing bowl combine cream cheese, Parmesan cheese, capers, milk, garlic and pepper; set aside.

Rinse chicken; pat dry. Place each breast half between 2 pieces of plastic wrap. Working from the center to the edges, pound the chicken lightly with the flat side of a meat mallet to a 1/8 in/3 mm thickness. Remove the plastic wrap. Spread one fourth of the cream cheese mixture over each breast half. Fold in the sides and roll up jelly-roll style, pressing the edges to seal.

In a large frying pan heat the olive oil or cooking oil. Brown the chicken on both sides (about 5 minutes total). Transfer the chicken to a 2 qt/2 l baking dish. Pour the wine over the chicken. Bake, uncovered, in a preheated 350°F/180°C/Gas Mark 4 oven for 20 to 25 minutes, or until the chicken is tender and no pink remains.

Meanwhile, for red pepper coulis, in a blender container or food processor bowl blend or process roasted bell peppers until smooth; set aside. In a small saucepan heat remaining olive oil or cooking oil. Add garlic; cook and stir until tender but not brown. Add puréed roasted bell pepper, half-and-half (half cream) or light (single) cream, anchovy paste and capers. Heat through. To serve, spoon coulis onto 4 dinner plates and top with sliced chicken breasts.

*For an elegant appearance,
arrange slices of stuffed
chicken breasts in a pinwheel
pattern on top of the sauce;
decorate with clusters of asparagus
tips and shredded lemon peel.*

BROILING
AND GRILLING

Broiling Chicken

Broiling and grilling are basic methods that are well suited to cooking chicken because they showcase its versatility. They are essentially identical techniques. While grilling (sometimes called barbecuing in Europe) is usually done out of doors and broiling (known in Europe as grilling) is done in the kitchen, both utilize dry, radiant heat. The main difference is that in most cases the heat in broiling comes from the top while in grilling it comes from beneath.

In some ways, broiling is even simpler than grilling because it requires no special equipment other than a broiler pan with a rack, and because a broiler is built into most home ovens. For broiling, however, as with grilling, a delicate balance of time and distance from the heat must be coordinated to produce a deliciously juicy end result: food that is nicely browned on the outside and the proper doneness within. The trick is to know how far away from the heating element to set the oven rack and broiler pan. As a rule, because they take longer to cook through, bone-in pieces need more distance, about 5 to 6 in/13 to 15 cm, than quick-cooking boneless cuts or kabobs, which should be cooked about 4 in/10 cm from the heat.

BASIC TOOLS FOR BROILING

broiler pan with rack

measuring cup

pastry brush

ruler

Use a broiler pan with a slotted rack, a ruler to measure the distance between the heating element and the food's surface and a cup and brush for basting. (For easier cleaning, you may want to line the broiler pan with aluminum foil.)

Try to broil chicken pieces that are similar in size so that they cook in the same amount of time.

STEP 1

Arranging Chicken on Pan

If chicken pieces have been marinated, lift them from the marinade and let them drain slightly. Arrange the chicken pieces skin-side down on the unheated broiler rack, then set the pan on the oven rack.

Most ovens come with a broiler pan, but if you need to purchase one, the rack should be slotted so that grease drips into the pan below.

STEP 2

Measuring Distance from Heat

Always measure from the heating element to the surface of the food. Most cuts should be broiled 4 to 6 in/10 to 15 cm from the heat; adjust the height of the oven rack, if necessary. Preheat the broiler according to the manufacturer's directions.

Pull the oven rack with the broiler pan out of the oven when basting to keep your hands safe from the heat.

Baste evenly, saving some of the sauce to brush on just before serving, if desired.

STEP 3

Basting Chicken

Broil the chicken completely on its underside before basting. Turn the pieces with long-handled tongs to protect your hands, then brush with the marinade or glaze as directed in the recipe.

Unlike grilling, broiling imparts no flavor of its own to food. Some seasoning, in the form of herbs, a marinade or a baste, is required to transform what could be a bland dish into one that is full of flavor. Brush on a simple sauce or marinade, such as the honey-soy glaze on page 105, and the taste of broiled chicken changes dramatically.

Grilling Chicken

Chicken is ideal for grilling. We never tire of the smoky essence that infuses its mild-flavored meat or of the wonderful aroma as it cooks to a crispy turn. Chicken cooked over hot coals is not only full of flavor, it also suits today's health-conscious cooking because grilling is a dry-heat method that requires little added fat.

Whether you use a simple grate or an elaborate barbecue kettle, the goal is the same: to balance time and temperature so that the food is moist and tender. But a good grill cook also depends on visual clues: Is the food cooking evenly? Should it be turned so that it won't burn? Grilling is very interactive; it requires your attention. That's what makes it fun to do and to watch.

The steps on these pages demonstrate how to start a charcoal fire correctly for both direct- and indirect-heat cooking. Your recipe will specify which method to use. Always preheat the upper grill rack over the ash-gray coals for a few minutes and brush it with oil so food won't stick to it. Afterwards, scrape it clean with a wire brush for the same reason.

Grilled recipes in this book are also suitable for gas grills. Use the same temperatures for both charcoal and gas grills.

BASIC TOOLS FOR GRILLING

drip pan

charcoal

long tongs

basting brush

long matches

Fire up the grill with charcoal briquettes and long matches; use long-handled tongs and a basting brush to keep your hands away from the fire. A drip pan is used for indirect-heat grilling.

89

Broiling and Grilling

Use enough briquettes so that when spread out in a single layer, they will extend slightly beyond the cooking area.

STEP I

Lighting Charcoal

Arrange the charcoal briquettes in a pyramid in the center of the lower grill rack. If they are self-lighting, ignite them with a match. If they are regular briquettes, use an electric starter or chimney device, or squirt them with lighter fluid and then ignite. The briquettes are ready when covered with a gray ash: 30 to 40 minutes for regular, 5 to 10 minutes for self-lighting.

Use the direct-heat method for grilling smaller chicken pieces.

STEP 2

Briquettes for Direct Heat

For direct-heat grilling, use long-handled tongs and spread the hot coals in a single layer across the grate. Food will cook more evenly if the coals are arranged with about 1/2 in/12 mm of space between each briquette.

Use the
indirect-heat
method for
grilling whole
or butterflied
chicken.

STEP 3

Briquettes for Indirect Heat
For indirect-heat grilling, arrange the hot coals around
the edge of the grill, leaving a space in the center. Set
a disposable foil drip pan in the middle so that it is
surrounded by briquettes. The food is placed on the
upper grill rack over the drip pan, then the grill is
covered so that heat and smoke circulate evenly.

Hold your hand
in the center of
the grill above the
coals or pan.

STEP 4

Testing Heat of Coals
Check the temperature by holding your hand, palm-side
down, at about the height at which the food will cook.
If you must pull your hand away after 2 seconds, the
coals are hot; 3 seconds, medium hot; 4 seconds,
medium; 5 seconds, medium slow; 6 seconds, slow.
When grilling with indirect heat, the temperature of
the coals should be one level hotter than the desired
temperature over the drip pan.

Broiling and Grilling

STEP 5

Brushing Meat with Marinade

Use a long-handled basting brush to coat the chicken with marinade. Marinades containing raw meat juices should be thoroughly cooked on the meat, so be sure to cook the chicken at least 5 minutes more after the last time you brush it with the marinade. Or, cook the marinade by bringing it to boiling before brushing it onto the meat.

Chicken pieces soaked in the same tangy citrus marinade used for a butterflied chicken (page 99) are grilled to a golden brown for a juicy, light main course or lunch dish.

About Marinades

Marinades serve two purposes; they are an easy way to add extra flavor to meat, poultry and fish and, if they contain an acidic ingredient such as citrus juice, wine or vinegar, they also help to tenderize the more inexpensive cuts of meat. The longer the marination time, the more tender and flavorsome the result. Eight hours or overnight gives the best results, but even an hour's marinating will be effective.

sage

Mix the marinade ingredients thoroughly. Place the meat, poultry or fish in a glass or ceramic dish and add the marinade, turning the meat to coat it well. (If the marinade contains an acidic ingredient such as wine or citrus juice, don't use metal dishes as the acid will react with the metal and produce an unpleasant taste.) Drain the meat before cooking it, but retain any leftover marinade; it can be used as a baste when the meat is cooking. Marinades containing raw meat juices must be cooked thoroughly to kill bacteria that could transmit disease. When basting with a marinade, cook it on the meat for at least five minutes after the last time the meat is basted. Alternatively, boil the marinade for a few minutes. It can then also be served as a dipping sauce, if desired.

Choose marinade ingredients that complement the flavor of the dish. Stronger-flavored meats can take more robust marinades, but chicken needs a more subtle marinade that will enhance but not overwhelm its milder taste. When using a marinade that contains sugar or honey, cook the meat on a lower temperature than usual to prevent the marinade burning. You may need to increase the cooking time to compensate for the lower temperature.

Chicken Breasts with Tomato–Mint Pesto

For a more Italian flavor, omit the lemon pepper
and use fresh basil leaves instead of the mint.
This pesto is also a tasty accompaniment to lamb or pork.

INGREDIENTS

1/3 cup/1/2 oz/15 g packed fresh
mint leaves

1/3 cup/1/2 oz/15 g packed fresh
parsley sprigs with stems removed

1/3 cup/1 oz/30 g dried tomatoes

1/4 cup/2 fl oz/60 ml olive oil

1 clove garlic, halved

1 1/2 teaspoons finely
shredded lemon peel

1/4 teaspoon salt

1/8 teaspoon lemon–pepper
seasoning

4 medium chicken breast halves
(1 lb/500 g total)

Preparation time 20 minutes
Broiling time 25 to 35 minutes
Makes 4 servings

*All you need to round out a meal of
broiled chicken stuffed with pesto is a
side dish of orzo pasta or rice pilaf.*

Broiling and Grilling

In a blender container or food processor bowl combine mint leaves, parsley, dried tomatoes, olive oil, garlic, lemon peel, salt and lemon–pepper seasoning. Cover and blend or process until finely chopped. Set aside.

If desired, remove skin from chicken. Cut a pocket in each chicken breast half by cutting a 2-in/5-cm-deep slit just above the breastbone on the meaty side of the breast. Fill each pocket with one fourth of the pesto.

Place breasts, bone-side up, on the unheated rack of the broiler pan. Broil 4 to 5 in/10 to 13 cm from the heat for 20 minutes. Turn chicken and broil for 5 to 15 minutes more, or until tender and no pink remains.

STEPS FOR MAKING POCKETS

Broiling and Grilling

STEP 1

Cutting Pockets

Place a chicken breast half on the cutting board skin-side up. With a small knife or boning knife, make a pocket 2 in/5 cm deep and about 3 in/7.5 cm long in the breastbone side of the meat.

STEP 2

Filling Pockets

Combine all ingredients for pesto filling in a blender or food processor. Hold open the pocket of one breast half and spoon in one fourth of the pesto mixture. Repeat with remaining breast halves and filling.

Citrus-soaked butterflied chicken makes a delicious and impressive-looking main course for a barbecue.

Butterflied Citrus Chicken

Butterflying chicken allows the maximum amount of surface area to be exposed
to the grill. Use the indirect-heat method, as shown on page 91.
The coals are medium hot when you can hold your hand above them for just 3 seconds.

INGREDIENTS

2¹/₂ to 3 lb/1.25 to 1.5 kg whole
broiler-fryer (roasting) chicken

¹/₃ cup/2¹/₂ fl oz/80 ml olive oil
or cooking oil

¹/₃ cup/2¹/₂ fl oz/80 ml
orange juice

¹/₄ cup/2 fl oz/60 ml lemon juice

1¹/₂ teaspoons dried rosemary,
crushed

2 cloves garlic, minced

¹/₂ teaspoon salt

¹/₄ teaspoon pepper

Preparation time 30 minutes
Marinating time 8 to 24 hours
Grilling time 60 to 70 minutes
Makes 4 servings

Use poultry or kitchen shears to cut closely along both sides of the backbone for the entire length of the chicken. Discard backbone. Turn skin-side up and open the bird out as flat as possible. Cover with clear plastic wrap. Strike breast firmly in the center with the flat side of a meat mallet. (This breaks the breastbone so the bird lies flat.) Twist wing tips under the back. Halfway between the legs and breastbone near the tip of the breast, cut a 1-in/2.5-cm slit through the skin on either side of and parallel with the breastbone. Insert drumstick tips into the slits. Place butterflied chicken in a large baking dish.

In a small mixing bowl stir together olive oil or cooking oil, orange juice, lemon juice, rosemary, garlic, salt and pepper. Pour into a large plastic bag; add chicken. Seal bag; turn bag to coat chicken with marinade. Marinate in the refrigerator for 8 to 24 hours, turning bag occasionally. Drain marinade from chicken, reserving marinade.

In a covered grill arrange medium-hot coals on the grate around a drip pan, then test for medium heat above the pan. Place chicken, skin-side up, on the grill rack directly over the drip pan, not over the coals. Brush with some of the reserved marinade. Cover and grill for 30 minutes. Brush with additional marinade. Grill for 30 to 40 minutes more, or until chicken is tender and no pink remains. Discard remaining marinade.

The backbone, along with other chicken offcuts, can be kept for making stock.

STEP 1
Removing Backbone
Set the bird on the cutting board breast-side down. With kitchen scissors or poultry shears, cut closely along one side of the backbone, then the other; discard backbone.

STEP 2
Flattening Bird
Turn the chicken skin-side up with the breast facing you, wings up, legs down. Open the bird as flat as possible. Cover with a large sheet of plastic wrap. Flatten by striking the breast firmly in the center with the smooth side of a meat mallet to break the breastbone.

STEP 3
Tucking Legs into Slits
Halfway between the legs and breastbone, near the bottom tip of the breast, cut a 1-in/2.5-cm slit through the loose skin on either side of and parallel with the breastbone. Insert the tips of the drumsticks into the slits to secure them so they won't pop up during grilling.

Japanese Chicken Kabobs

**When weather permits, cook the kabobs on the grill instead of the broiler.
As a main course, serve the kabobs on a bed of fluffy steamed white rice.
Serve these as appetizers, too—warm or chilled. Allow 1 kabob per serving.**

INGREDIENTS

1 teaspoon finely shredded orange peel

1/2 cup/4 fl oz/125 ml orange juice

1/3 cup/2 1/2 fl oz/80 ml dry sherry

1/4 cup/2 fl oz/60 ml soy sauce

2 teaspoons sugar

1 clove garlic, minced

1/2 teaspoon grated ginger root

12 oz/375 g boneless, skinless chicken breast halves

6 to 8 green (spring) onions

Hot cooked rice

Pickled ginger (optional)

Preparation time 40 minutes
Marinating time 30 minutes
Broiling time 8 to 10 minutes
Makes 4 servings

STEPS AT A GLANCE	Page
■ Skinning and boning	19–21
■ Broiling chicken	86–87

Garnish this dish with Japanese flair by folding several slices of pickled ginger into a rose shape. To make green onion spirals, thinly slice the tops lengthwise and float them in ice water until they curl.

103

Soak twelve 6-in/15-cm wooden skewers in water for 30 minutes. In a small mixing bowl combine the orange peel, orange juice, sherry, soy sauce, sugar, garlic and ginger root. Set aside ¼ cup/2 fl oz/ 60 ml of the marinade mixture to serve with the cooked kabobs.

Cut chicken breast halves into 1-in/2.5-cm pieces. Cut green (spring) onions into 1½-in/4-cm lengths. Thread 3 chicken pieces and 2 onion pieces onto each wooden skewer, alternating chicken and onions. Place kabobs in a shallow dish and pour marinade over them. Marinate at room temperature for 30 minutes, turning kabobs once. Remove kabobs from marinade, reserving marinade.

Preheat broiler. Place kabobs on the unheated rack of a broiler pan. Broil 4 in/10 cm from the heat for 8 to 10 minutes, or until chicken is tender and no pink remains, turning and brushing with reserved marinade once.

Meanwhile, heat the ¼ cup/2 fl oz/60 ml reserved marinade. Serve with kabobs, rice and pickled ginger, if desired.

Honey-Glazed Drumsticks

These sweet, deliciously sticky drumsticks
will encourage even the most polite diners to lick their fingers,
so supply plenty of napkins with this hands-on meal.

INGREDIENTS

¹/₄ cup/2 fl oz/60 ml honey

2 tablespoons soy sauce

1 tablespoon cider vinegar

1 tablespoon molasses (optional)

8 chicken drumsticks
(about 2¹/₄ lb/1.125 kg total)

Preparation time 15 minutes
Broiling time 25 to 30 minutes
Makes 4 servings

STEPS AT A GLANCE	Page
▦ Broiling chicken	86–87

A display of brightly colored napkins and a bouquet of fresh herbs set off tantalizing drumsticks.

In a small saucepan combine the honey, soy sauce, vinegar and, if desired, molasses. Cook over medium-low heat for about 5 minutes, or until bubbly, stirring occasionally. (Watch mixture closely, as it will foam.)

Meanwhile, preheat broiler. If desired, remove skin from chicken. Rinse chicken; pat dry. Place on a rack in an unheated broiler pan.

Broil 5 to 6 in/13 to 15 cm from the heat for about 15 minutes, or until chicken is light brown. Turn chicken and broil for 10 to 15 minutes more, or until chicken is tender and no pink remains. Brush chicken with glaze once more during the last 5 to 10 minutes of broiling. Before serving, spoon any remaining glaze over the drumsticks.

Chicken Salad Niçoise

**This salad is a delicious twist on a French classic.
We've used chicken instead of the customary tuna.**

INGREDIENTS

SALAD DRESSING

12 oz/375 g bottled or tinned
marinated artichoke hearts

2 tablespoons balsamic vinegar

1 tablespoon drained capers

1 tablespoon anchovy paste

1 tablespoon Dijon-style mustard

4 cloves garlic, minced

1/2 teaspoon Herbes de Provence
or dried thyme leaves

SALAD

12 oz/375 g boneless, skinless
chicken breast halves

Spinach or romaine (cos)
lettuce leaves

8 tiny new potatoes, cooked and
quartered

2 medium tomatoes,
cut into wedges

1 medium green and/or red bell
pepper (capsicum), cut into strips

2 hard-cooked eggs, sliced

1 fresh fennel bulb, sliced

1/4 cup/1 oz/30 g Niçoise
or Kalamata olives or pitted
ripe olives

*Capture the sunny tastes
of Provençal cuisine with
this summertime salad.*

Broiling and Grilling

Preparation time 35 minutes
Marinating time 8 to 24 hours
Broiling time 12 to 16 minutes
Makes 4 servings

For salad dressing, drain artichokes, reserving liquid. In a screw-top jar combine the reserved artichoke liquid, vinegar, capers, anchovy paste, mustard, garlic and herbes de Provence or dried thyme leaves. Shake well.

For salad, in a large plastic bag combine chicken breast halves and ¼ cup/2 fl oz/60 ml of the salad dressing. (Cover and chill the remaining salad dressing until serving time.) Seal bag and turn to coat chicken with dressing. Marinate in the refrigerator for 8 to 24 hours. Drain marinade from chicken; discard marinade.

Preheat broiler. Place chicken on the unheated rack of a broiler pan. Broil 5 to 6 in/13 to 15 cm from the heat for 6 to 8 minutes per side, or until chicken is tender and no pink remains. Cool slightly, then slice each chicken breast diagonally. Line a large serving platter with spinach or romaine (cos) lettuce leaves. Arrange the chicken, artichokes, potatoes, tomatoes, bell pepper strips, eggs, fennel and olives on the platter. Drizzle the remaining dressing over the salad just before serving.

About Vinegar

The word "vinegar" comes from the French *vin aigre*, or sour wine. Souring occurs naturally when alcohol reacts with airborne bacteria to produce a thick, mouldy-looking skin on the surface of the liquid. This layer of bacteria and yeasts cells converts the alcohol into acetic acid, which is what gives vinegar its characteristic sharpness. Vinegar can also be made from other alcohol-based liquids, such as malt, cider or rice wine.

The quality of the vinegar depends on that of the raw ingredients. Stronger, coarser vinegars, such as spirit and malt vinegars, are used mostly for pickling. Some of the best vinegars are made from fine wines such as Rioja, Champagne and sherry. One of the most costly, balsamic vinegar, is made from unfermented grape juice that is aged in wooden casks for at least 5 years; some have been aged for 150 years. Like wine, balsamic vinegar continues to mature in the bottle.

Vinegar is often used to preserve foods, especially fruit and vegetables, but it is also a very versatile flavoring. Cider vinegar marries well with pork; wine or balsamic vinegars go surprisingly well with soft fruits such as berries, and are ideal for salad dressings and mayonnaise. Tarragon vinegar complements chicken; a touch of spiced vinegar enhances game. Vinegars flavored with fruits, herbs or spices can be bought ready-made, or easily made at home from good-quality wine vinegar and fresh, ripe fruits or unblemished herbs. Stored in a cool, dark place, vinegar will keep indefinitely.

When you need an elegant dish in
a hurry, slice or shred the meat
from a purchased broiled or
grilled chicken to make
a gourmet fast food
version of this salad.

Chicken, Avocado and Mango Salad

A creamy curry and macadamia dressing gives a tropical taste to this rich but simple summertime salad.

INGREDIENTS

SALAD DRESSING

3 tablespoons olive oil

1 onion, finely chopped

2 teaspoons curry powder

1 tablespoon apricot jelly or jam

1 tablespoon mango chutney

1/4 cup/1 oz/30 g unsalted macadamia nuts

2 tablespoons raspberry vinegar

1/2 cup/4 fl oz/125 ml mayonnaise

1/4 cup/2 fl oz/60 ml light (single) cream

SALAD

4 skinless, boneless, single chicken breasts, broiled

1 bunch/3 1/2 oz/100 g arugula (rocket), washed and stemmed

2 large mangoes, peeled, pitted and sliced

2 large avocados, peeled, pitted and sliced

1 bunch fresh chives, cut into 2 in/5 cm lengths, for garnish

Preparation time 30 minutes
Broiling time 20 to 30 minutes
Makes 4 servings

STEPS AT A GLANCE	Page
■ Skinning and boning	19–21
■ Broiling chicken	86–87

For salad dressing, heat 1 tablespoon of the olive oil over medium heat in a small saucepan. Add the onion and cook until translucent. Add the curry powder and cook, stirring, for 1 minute. Remove from the heat and stir in the apricot jelly or jam and mango chutney, mixing well. Set aside until cool.

In a blender or food processor, process the macadamia nuts briefly until chopped, add the remaining oil and the vinegar and process until well combined. Add the nut mixture to the cooled onion mixture. Stir in the mayonnaise and cream. Mix well.

Slice the cooked chicken breasts lengthwise into 5 or 6 strips. Arrange the arugula (rocket), chicken, mango and avocado on individual serving plates. Spoon some of the dressing over each serving.

Garnish with the chives and serve immediately.

Spicy Spanish Kabobs

Saffron, the hand-gathered stigmas from a variety of Mediterranean crocus, is the most costly spice in the world. Ground turmeric can be used in its place; it will change the flavor of the dish only slightly.

INGREDIENTS

1/4 cup/2 fl oz/60 ml olive oil or cooking oil

1 tablespoon lemon juice

2 tablespoons snipped fresh parsley

1/2 teaspoon ground cumin

1/4 to 1/2 teaspoon crushed red (chili) pepper flakes

1/2 teaspoon dried thyme, crushed

1/2 teaspoon paprika

1/8 teaspoon thread saffron, crushed

1/4 teaspoon salt

1/4 teaspoon black pepper

12 oz/375 g boneless, skinless chicken thighs, cut into 1-in/2.5-cm cubes or 2 x 1-in/ 5 x 2.5-cm strips

Preparation time 25 minutes
Marinating time 4 to 24 hours
Grilling time 10 to 12 minutes
Makes 4 servings

In a medium mixing bowl stir together olive oil or cooking oil, lemon juice, parsley, cumin, red (chili) pepper flakes, thyme, paprika, saffron, salt and black pepper. Pour into a plastic bag; add chicken pieces. Seal bag; turn to coat chicken with marinade. Marinate in the refrigerator for 4 to 24 hours, turning the bag occasionally. Drain marinade from chicken, reserving marinade.

Thread chicken pieces on 4 long metal skewers, leaving about 1/4 in/6 mm between pieces. Place chicken kabobs on the grill rack of an uncovered grill. Grill directly over medium coals for 10 to 12 minutes, or until chicken is tender and no pink remains, turning once and brushing occasionally with reserved marinade.

A bed of golden rice, flavored with saffron and peas, frames grilled Spanish-style brochettes.

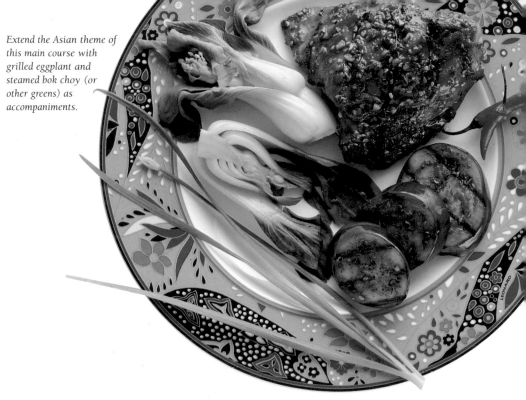

Extend the Asian theme of this main course with grilled eggplant and steamed bok choy (or other greens) as accompaniments.

Firecracker Chicken Thighs

Available in Asian markets and some supermarkets,
hot bean paste gives a tingling spiciness to this dish. To toast the sesame seeds,
place them in a shallow pan and bake in a preheated 350°F/180°C/Gas Mark 4 oven
for 3 to 5 minutes, or until golden.

INGREDIENTS

1 1/2 to 2 lb/750 g to 1 kg
chicken thighs

2 to 3 tablespoons
hot bean paste

2 tablespoons soy sauce

2 tablespoons toasted sesame
seeds, crushed

1 tablespoon toasted sesame oil

1 tablespoon sugar

1/4 cup/1 oz/30 g finely chopped
green (spring) onions

4 large cloves garlic, minced
(1 tablespoon)

1/4 teaspoon salt

1/8 teaspoon pepper

Broiling and Grilling

Preparation time 20 minutes
Marinating time 4 to 24 hours
Grilling time 30 to 35 minutes
Makes 4 to 6 servings

STEPS AT A GLANCE   Page
■ Skinning chicken thighs   19
■ Scoring and marinating
   chicken   241
■ Grilling chicken   90–92

Remove skin from chicken thighs. Score meat on both sides by making shallow diagonal cuts about 1 in/2.5 cm apart.

In a large mixing bowl stir together bean paste, soy sauce, sesame seeds, sesame oil, sugar, green (spring) onions, garlic, salt and pepper. Pour into a plastic bag; add chicken thighs. Seal bag; turn bag to coat chicken. Marinate in the refrigerator for 4 to 24 hours, turning bag occasionally. Remove chicken, scraping off excess marinade. Reserve marinade.

Place chicken on the grill rack of an uncovered grill. Grill directly over medium coals for 15 minutes. Turn chicken over and grill for 10 to 15 minutes more. Baste both sides with reserved marinade and grill for 5 minutes more, or until chicken is tender and no pink remains, turning once. Discard any remaining marinade.

About Sesame Seeds and Oil

Sesame is an annual plant, reaching about 6½ feet/2 m in height, which is grown for its seeds. It is a very old crop; it probably originated in Africa, but was first cultivated in ancient Persia, from where it was introduced to the Middle East, India and the rest of Asia. It has been extensively grown in China and India for hundreds of years, and is now cultivated worldwide in tropical and subtropical climates, and even in some Mediterranean countries.

Sesame is widely used in Asian and Middle Eastern cookery. The seeds are sprinkled on cakes and breads, added to rice dishes, ground into a paste to produce tahina or made into the Turkish sweetmeat halva. Sesame seeds can also be cold pressed to extract their oil. The seeds may be toasted first; oil from toasted seeds is darker in color and has a more pronounced flavor. Sesame oil makes a pleasantly nutty, distinctive addition to salad dressings, stir-fries and marinades, especially when an Asian flavor is called for.

Because of its strong flavor and low burning point, sesame oil is more commonly used as a flavoring oil rather than a cooking oil. If used for frying, it is best combined with a less combustible oil such as canola, safflower or blended vegetable oil. Like all nut and seed oils, sesame oil becomes rancid quickly, especially in warm climates. It is best bought in small quantities, stored in the refrigerator and used as soon as possible.

FRYING AND SAUTÉING

Pan-Frying Chicken

Pan-frying uses a small amount of fat, as opposed to deep-frying, which uses much more. Chicken cooked this way is juicy and flavorful, with a browned, crunchy exterior that is not at all greasy. To provide a barrier between the food and the cooking fat, pan-fried foods are usually coated in flour, then in a liquid such as milk, then again in either flour or bread-crumbs, or just dipped in liquid and floured. These layers add texture, flavor and color.

Temperature control makes the difference between pan-fried chicken that is browned and chicken that is burnt or unevenly cooked. For the best results, select a frying pan with a heavy bottom that is responsive to changes in temperature, retains heat and conducts it evenly. The pan should be large enough so you can cook a number of pieces in it at a time, with a handle that stays cool and is comfortable to hold. For safety, always turn the handle away from you so that you don't accidentally knock against it and spill the hot fat.

BASIC TOOLS FOR PAN-FRYING

For pan-frying, use a pie plate and a plastic bag to hold the coatings and a heavy frying pan and tongs for cooking chicken.

pie plate

large frying pan

plastic bag

tongs

STEPS FOR PAN-FRYING CHICKEN

Use a plastic bag to coat several chicken pieces at a time in the flour mixture.

STEP 1

Coating Chicken Pieces

First dredge the chicken in flour so that the liquid has something to adhere to. Pour the buttermilk or other liquid into a pie plate and dip the flour-coated chicken in the buttermilk, then again in the flour mixture.

Frying and Sautéing

Leave room between the pieces so that all sides of the chicken are exposed to the cooking oil.

STEP 2

Adding Chicken Pieces to Oil

Add the oil to the frying pan and set the temperature to medium. When the fat is hot, place the coated chicken pieces in the pan with tongs and cook until the first side is evenly browned, about 15 minutes.

Handle the pieces carefully when you turn them so that the coating stays intact.

STEP 3

Turning Chicken in Frying Pan

Once the pieces are nicely browned on one side, turn them to brown the other side. Reduce the heat to medium low and cook until the chicken is tender.

*Succulent Crispy Fried Chicken
(page 141) is the ultimate picnic
food or the much-appreciated
centerpiece of a family supper.*

127

Sautéing Chicken

Cooking foods quickly in a small amount of fat until nicely browned on the outside and tender and juicy within is the method known as sautéing. Most bone-in cuts of chicken are sautéed only as a first step in braising (see page 228), but boneless chicken breasts or thighs are superb when cooked in this fashion and served with an easy-to-make pan sauce.

When a recipe calls for boneless, skinless chicken, see pages 19–21 to do your own boning and skinning, or buy the pieces already prepared. If desired, flatten each piece of chicken with a mallet (as shown on page 46) to maximize the surface area and ensure even cooking. For a crisp crust that locks in moisture, dredge the chicken in seasoned flour before cooking (this step is not always necessary when sautéing). To finish, deglaze the pan with juice, stock or wine, then stir in seasonings to taste.

Once you are comfortable with sautéing, you can prepare an elegant party meal very quickly. It is an ideal method for impromptu dinners because it requires very little preparation, especially if your pantry is stocked with flour, seasonings and deglazing liquids and your freezer has a supply of chicken breasts or thighs.

BASIC TOOLS FOR SAUTÉING CHICKEN

To successfully sauté chicken pieces, you need only a roomy frying pan, a measuring cup, tongs, a wooden spoon and a shallow plate.

large frying pan

measuring cup

shallow plate

tongs

wooden spoon

STEPS FOR SAUTÉING CHICKEN

If the flour is unseasoned, sprinkle the chicken first with salt and pepper to flavor it before dredging it with the flour.

STEP 1

Coating Chicken with Flour

Place flour on a plate. Hold the chicken (in this case, a boneless, skinless breast half) at one end and lay it across the flour to coat. Lift the meat, turn it and place it in the flour again to coat the other side.

Frying and Sautéing

Turn the chicken with long-handled tongs so splatters don't burn your hand.

STEP 2

Sautéing Chicken Pieces

Heat oil or butter in the pan. When the bubbles subside, add the chicken and cook until golden brown; turn and cook on the other side until it is evenly browned on the surface and opaque within. Transfer to a warm serving platter.

Stir with a wooden spoon, which won't get as hot as a metal utensil.

STEP 3

Deglazing Pan

Slowly pour the cold liquid into the hot pan to dislodge the browned bits left on the bottom when the chicken was browned. Stir and boil to concentrate the flavors of the sauce.

Reducing the liquid
thickens the sauce
and intensifies
its flavor.

STEP 4

Thickening Sauce

Let the sauce cook until some of the liquid is evaporated
and the volume is reduced to about half the original
amount. Taste before serving and adjust the seasonings,
if necessary.

*To serve, return the cooked chicken
to the pan with the sauce to reheat it
quickly, then transfer to a plate and
drizzle with the sauce. The recipe for
this classic dish, Sherried Chicken
with Orange Sauce, appears
on page 160.*

Create a succulent dinner featuring chicken in a rich butter sauce, sautéed baby squash and cherry tomatoes and roasted thinly sliced potatoes.

Sautéed Breasts with Beurre Blanc

Beurre blanc, a classic French sauce, breaks down easily
and cannot be reheated. If it turns oily, beat a spoonful of it in a chilled bowl
until creamy, then add the rest of the sauce a spoonful at a time.

INGREDIENTS

4 boneless, skinless chicken breast halves (1 lb/500 g total)

1 tablespoon olive oil or cooking oil

Salt

Pepper

2 tablespoons finely chopped shallots or green (spring) onion

1/4 cup/2 fl oz/60 ml sherry wine vinegar or white wine vinegar

1/4 cup/2 fl oz/60 ml dry sherry

1 tablespoon heavy (double) cream

3 oz/90 g butter (at room temperature), cut into 6 pieces

1/8 teaspoon white pepper

METHOD FOR MAKING SAUTÉED BREASTS WITH BEURRE BLANC

Preparation time 15 minutes
Cooking time 10 to 12 minutes
Makes 4 servings

Rinse chicken; pat dry. In a large frying pan, heat oil over medium heat. Add chicken and cook for 10 to 12 minutes, or until tender and no pink remains, turning once. Sprinkle chicken with salt and pepper.

Meanwhile, in a small heavy saucepan combine shallots or green (spring) onion, vinegar and dry sherry. Bring to boiling; boil, uncovered, for about 4 minutes, or until about 1 tablespoon of liquid remains.

With a wire whisk, whisk in cream and boil gently for 2 to 3 minutes, or until thickened. Remove pan from heat. Whisk in butter 1 piece at a time, allowing butter to melt completely before adding the next piece of butter. Season to taste with white pepper. If desired, strain the sauce to remove chopped shallots. Serve immediately over chicken.

STEP 1

Adding Butter

After boiling down the shallot mixture and adding the cream, boil the sauce gently for 2 to 3 minutes to thicken. Remove from the heat and whisk in the first piece of butter. Incorporate each piece of butter completely before adding the next.

STEP 2

Finishing Sauce

As the butter is blended into the sauce mixture, the sauce becomes silken and smooth. Remember to incorporate each piece of butter completely before adding the next; this keeps the sauce at the right consistency. Season with pepper, strain to remove the shallots, if desired, then spoon sauce over the chicken.

Chicken Provençal

For a light main dish, these chicken breasts are served with an earthy vegetable stew. The meat is cooked in minimal oil and the vegetables are steamed in wine.

INGREDIENTS

10 oz/300 g cubed peeled eggplant (aubergine)

2 medium tomatoes, peeled, seeded and chopped

1 medium onion, halved and thinly sliced

1 medium red bell pepper (capsicum), cut into thin strips

1 medium green bell pepper (capsicum), cut into thin strips

1/4 cup/2 fl oz/60 ml red or dry white wine or chicken stock

2 tablespoons snipped fresh basil or 1 1/2 teaspoons dried basil, crushed

2 cloves garlic, minced

1/2 teaspoon salt

4 boneless, skinless chicken breast halves (1 lb/500g total)

Salt (extra)

1 tablespoon olive oil or cooking oil

1/2 teaspoon paprika

This ratatouille-like dish is ideal on a warm summer's evening. All it needs is some crusty bread and a crisp salad drizzled with vinaigrette.

METHOD FOR MAKING CHICKEN PROVENÇAL

Preparation time 30 minutes
Cooking time 20 minutes
Makes 4 servings

In a large saucepan combine the eggplant (aubergine), tomatoes, onion, bell peppers (capsicum), wine or chicken stock, basil, garlic and 1/2 teaspoon salt. Bring to boiling; reduce heat. Simmer, covered, for 10 minutes. Uncover and simmer for 5 minutes more, or until vegetables are tender and nearly all of the liquid is evaporated.

Meanwhile, rinse chicken; pat dry. Place each breast half between 2 pieces of plastic wrap. Working from the center to the edges, pound chicken lightly with the flat side of a meat mallet to a 1/4-in/6-mm thickness. Remove plastic wrap. Sprinkle chicken lightly with extra salt.

In a large frying pan heat the oil and paprika over medium-high heat. Add the chicken and cook for 4 to 6 minutes, or until tender and no pink remains, turning once. To serve, spoon vegetables onto plates and top with chicken.

STEPS FOR PREPARING TOMATOES AND HERBS

STEP 1

Peeling Tomatoes
With a sharp knife, cut an X at the bottom of the tomato. Plunge the tomato into boiling water for 30 seconds; remove and cool in ice water, then drain. To peel, pull back one segment of skin at the X. Repeat with remaining skin.

STEP 2

Seeding Tomatoes
After peeling, cut the tomato in half crosswise between the stem and blossom ends. Holding it upside down, gently squeeze each half to push out the seeds from the cavities. If some seeds remain, pick them out with a paring knife, grapefruit spoon or your fingers.

STEP 3

Snipping Fresh Basil
Put the basil leaves in a small measuring cup or ramekin. If the leaves are large, stack them first and cut them into pieces. With kitchen scissors, snip them to the appropriate size.

What could be better with fried chicken and gravy than a warm corn muffin and butter? Some sliced tomatoes would be appropriate on a summer menu, or hot vegetables in the winter.

Crispy Fried Chicken

Enjoy this tried-and-true favorite warm with gravy for a family supper
or chilled and plain for your next picnic. If making the chicken ahead of time,
be sure to refrigerate it until it's cold and transport it in an iced container.

INGREDIENTS

CHICKEN

1 cup/4 oz/125 g all-purpose
(plain) flour

1 1/2 teaspoons dried basil,
crushed

1/2 teaspoon salt

1/2 teaspoon onion powder

1/4 teaspoon pepper

3 to 3 1/2 lb/1.5 to 1.75 kg whole
broiler-fryer (roasting) chicken,
cut up

1/2 cup/4 fl oz/125 ml buttermilk

2 tablespoons cooking oil

GRAVY

2 tablespoons all-purpose
(plain) flour

1 teaspoon instant chicken
bouillon (stock) granules

1/8 teaspoon pepper

1 3/4 cups/14 fl oz/430 ml milk

METHOD FOR MAKING CRISPY FRIED CHICKEN

Preparation time 15 minutes
Cooking time 50 to 55 minutes
Makes 6 servings

STEPS AT A GLANCE	Page
■ Pan-frying chicken	126

For chicken, in a plastic bag combine flour, basil, salt, onion powder and pepper. Set aside. If desired, remove skin from chicken. Rinse chicken; pat dry. Add chicken pieces 2 or 3 at a time to plastic bag, shaking bag to coat chicken pieces with flour mixture. Dip pieces, one at a time, into buttermilk. Add again to plastic bag with flour mixture, shaking to coat well.

In a 12-in/30-cm frying pan cook the chicken in hot oil for 15 minutes over medium heat, turning to brown evenly. Reduce heat to medium-low and cook, uncovered, for 35 to 40 minutes more, or until chicken is tender and no pink remains, turning occasionally. Remove chicken from frying pan; drain on paper towels. Transfer chicken to a serving platter; keep warm.

For gravy, stir flour, bouillon (stock) granules and pepper into drippings in frying pan, scraping up any browned bits. Add milk all at once. Cook and stir over medium heat until thickened and bubbly. Cook and stir for 1 minute more. Serve gravy with chicken.

About Basil

A member of the mint family, basil is an annual bush that grows to about 30 in/75 cm. It bears creamy white or purple-tinged flowers and tender, curved, veined leaves that have a distinctive, pungent flavor. There are several varieties, varying in color, size and flavor, and all can be used for culinary purposes.

Basil is one of the most important of the culinary herbs, a fact reflected in its name, which comes from the Greek *basilikon phyton*, or "kingly herb". It was known in ancient Greece, Rome and Egypt, and was introduced to Europe in the 16th century. Its greatest importance is in Italy, where it features in salads and pasta sauces and, most famously, in *pesto alla genovese*, a sauce made of basil, pine nuts, garlic, olive oil and parmesan cheese.

Basil has a particular affinity for tomatoes, but also tastes good with or in chicken dishes, soups, stews, mushroom dishes, zucchini (courgettes), fish, and egg and rice dishes. When buying fresh basil, look for glossy, green, unbruised leaves with a strong scent. Fresh basil should be kept in water in the refrigerator and used within two or three days. Dried basil has a different, more minty taste than fresh; rather than using dried basil, it is preferable to preserve fresh leaves. Freeze chopped leaves with a little water in ice cube trays; when frozen, release the cubes and store them in plastic bags in the freezer. Alternatively, preserve them in the Italian way: fill a jar with the leaves, lightly salt them and top the jar up with olive oil. Close the jar tightly and store in the refrigerator.

Oven-roasted new potatoes and steamed broccoli flank fried chicken for a simple, homey dinner.

Tangy Marinated Fried Chicken

Resist the temptation to save a few calories
and leave the skin on this chicken. It crisps up nicely
and turns a beautiful brown for a lovely appearance.

INGREDIENTS

MARINADE

4 cloves garlic

1/2 teaspoon salt

1/3 cup/2 1/2 fl oz/80 ml lime juice

2 tablespoons olive oil or
cooking oil

2 tablespoons water

1 teaspoon ground cumin

1/4 teaspoon ground turmeric

1/4 teaspoon pepper

FRIED CHICKEN

2 to 2 1/2 lb/1 to 1.25 kg meaty
chicken pieces (breasts, thighs
and drumsticks)

1/4 cup/1 oz/30 g all-purpose
(plain) flour

2 tablespoons olive oil or
cooking oil

Preparation time 15 minutes
Marinating time 8 to 24 hours
Cooking time 40 to 50 minutes
Makes 4 servings

STEPS AT A GLANCE	Page
■ Marinating chicken	241
■ Pan-frying chicken	126

For marinade, use a mortar and pestle or a bowl and wooden spoon to mash the garlic with the salt until a paste is formed. In a small bowl combine the garlic–salt mixture, lime juice, 2 tablespoons olive oil or cooking oil, water, cumin, turmeric and pepper.

For fried chicken, rinse chicken; pat dry. Pour marinade into a plastic bag; add chicken pieces. Seal bag; turn bag to coat chicken with marinade. Marinate in the refrigerator for 8 to 24 hours, turning bag occasionally. Drain marinade from chicken; discard marinade. Pat chicken dry with paper towels.

Place flour in a clean plastic bag. Add chicken, 2 or 3 pieces at a time; shake bag to coat chicken with flour. In a large ovenproof frying pan heat 2 tablespoons olive oil or cooking oil. Add chicken and cook, uncovered, over medium-low heat for 10 to 15 minutes, turning to brown evenly. Spoon off fat. Transfer frying pan to a preheated 375°F/190°C/Gas Mark 4 oven. Bake, uncovered, for 30 to 35 minutes, or until chicken is tender and no pink remains.

Sautéed Chicken with Tomato Chutney

Chutney is a catch-all term used for
any number of pickled fruit or vegetable combinations.
Usually chutneys are highly spiced, as is this streamlined version.

INGREDIENTS

2 lb/1 kg chicken thighs, skinned,
if desired

1 tablespoon cooking oil

2 medium tomatoes, peeled,
seeded and chopped

2 tart cooking apples, chopped

1 jalapeño pepper (small hot
chili), seeded and finely chopped

1/4 cup/1 1/2 oz/45 g currants or
raisins

1/2 cup/2 1/2 oz/75 g chopped red
bell pepper (capsicum)

1/4 cup/2 oz/60 g
chopped onion

1/4 cup/2 fl oz/
60 ml cider vinegar

1 tablespoon sugar

2 teaspoons grated
ginger root

1/4 teaspoon salt

METHOD FOR MAKING SAUTÉED CHICKEN WITH TOMATO CHUTNEY

Preparation time 30 minutes
Cooking time 40 to 45 minutes
Makes 4 servings

STEPS AT A GLANCE	Page
■ Sautéing chicken	130

Rinse chicken; pat dry. In a large frying pan heat cooking oil over medium-high heat. Add chicken thighs and brown quickly on both sides. Spoon off fat.

In a large mixing bowl stir together tomatoes, apples, jalapeño (chili) pepper, currants or raisins, red bell pepper (capsicum), onion, vinegar, sugar, ginger root and salt. Add to the frying pan with the chicken. Bring to boiling; reduce heat. Cover and simmer for about 35 to 40 minutes, or until chicken is tender and no pink remains.

Remove chicken from frying pan; keep warm. Boil tomato–apple mixture, uncovered, for about 5 minutes, or until thickened. Serve with chicken.

The chutney served with this chicken is so chunky and fresh, it plays the role of a vegetable. Round the meal out with a starch, such as mashed potatoes.

Coated in a luscious coconut sauce, these drumsticks are irresistible on a bed of julienned vegetables, such as carrots, zucchini and red sweet peppers.

Coconut Chicken

Coconut milk gives this dish a creamy consistency and a mild but distinct flavor
unlike that of coconut in its many sweetened incarnations.
For more information on coconut milk, see pages 153 and 309.

INGREDIENTS

8 chicken drumsticks
(2 lb/1 kg total)

2 tablespoons cooking oil

1 medium onion, halved and
thinly sliced

1 teaspoon curry powder

1 teaspoon finely shredded
lemon peel

1 tablespoon lemon juice

1/4 teaspoon salt

1 1/4 cups/10 fl oz/310 ml canned
coconut milk (unsweetened)

1/4 cup/1 oz/30 g toasted
coconut

Preparation time 20 minutes
Cooking time 44 to 54 minutes
Makes 4 servings

STEPS AT A GLANCE	Page
■ Sautéing chicken	130

In a large frying pan brown the chicken drumsticks in hot oil for about 8 minutes, turning to brown evenly. Remove chicken from frying pan and set aside.

In the same pan cook the onion for 5 minutes, or until tender but not brown. Stir in the curry powder and cook for 1 minute. Stir in the lemon peel, lemon juice and salt. Carefully stir in the coconut milk. Bring mixture to boiling; return chicken to frying pan. Reduce heat and simmer, covered, for 30 to 40 minutes, or until chicken is tender and no pink remains, turning chicken once and stirring occasionally. Serve chicken sprinkled with toasted coconut.

About Coconut

Coconut palms are native to south-east Asia, and are an important product in the area's economy. The flesh and juice of coconuts are staple ingredients in cuisines of the region; the husks of the nuts are used to make cloth, rope and brushes; the trunk of the palm is used as a building material; and the leaves are used for thatching roofs.

When buying coconuts, choose heavy nuts with "eyes" that are not mouldy or dry; this may indicate that the coconut is bad. Shake the nut; you should be able to hear juice sloshing about inside. To crack the shell, pierce two of the eyes with a nail or screwdriver, and drain off the clear juice. Bang the nut on a hard floor or hit it all over with a hammer until it breaks into pieces, then use a small, sharp knife to pare away the thin brown skin from each piece. Fresh coconut pieces should be stored in the refrigerator, preferably in their own juice.

Coconut yields several edible products; the flesh can be eaten as is, grated to use in recipes or infused with water to produce coconut milk (not to be confused with the juice inside the nut). Coconut oil is used as a cooking fat in many coconut-growing areas. Palm sugar, a common ingredient in Asian cuisines, is made by boiling down the juice. Although commercial products such as desiccated coconut and canned coconut milk are widely available, those made from fresh coconut have a superior flavor and texture. Coconut goes well in both sweet foods, such as cakes, desserts or cookies, and savory recipes, especially highly spiced ones featuring chicken or prawns.

Chicken with Beer Barbecue Sauce

**Enjoy the flavor of barbecued chicken
without stoking up the grill! Just sauté chicken pieces instead,
then simmer them in a piquant sauce.**

INGREDIENTS

2 lb/1 kg chicken drumsticks
and/or thighs, skinned, if desired

1 tablespoon cooking oil

1 oz/30 g chopped onion

3/4 cup/6 fl oz/190 ml
sweet chili sauce

1/2 cup/4 fl oz/125 ml beer

2 tablespoons brown sugar

1/2 teaspoon ground cumin

1/2 teaspoon prepared mustard

1/8 teaspoon pepper

Few drops hot pepper sauce

Preparation time 15 minutes
Cooking time 42 to 53 minutes
Makes 4 servings

STEPS AT A GLANCE   Page

■ Skinning and boning   19–21
■ Sautéing chicken   130

Whole ears of fresh corn are a delicious complement to chicken pieces simmered in a spicy sauce.

Rinse chicken; pat dry. In a large frying pan heat oil. Add chicken and cook, uncovered, over medium heat for 10 to 15 minutes, turning to brown evenly. Drain off fat. Add the onion to chicken and cook for 2 to 3 minutes.

In a small mixing bowl combine the chili sauce, beer, brown sugar, cumin, mustard, pepper and hot pepper sauce. Pour the sauce over the chicken. Bring to boiling; reduce heat. Simmer, covered, for 20 minutes. Uncover and turn chicken. Simmer, uncovered, for 10 to 15 minutes more, or until chicken is tender and no pink remains. Transfer chicken to a serving platter; keep warm.

Skim excess fat off sauce in pan. If desired, simmer sauce, uncovered, to desired consistency. Pass sauce with meat.

Chicken Fajitas

Fajitas are easily made at home. Use tomatoes instead of tomatillos for more color.
Purchase an oval fajita pan, available in specialty cookware stores,
if you want to present these Tex-Mex style.

INGREDIENTS

12 oz/375 g boneless, skinless chicken breast halves, cut into 2- × 1/2-in/5-cm × 12-mm strips

1/4 cup/2 fl oz/60 ml cooking oil

1/4 cup/2 fl oz/60 ml lime juice

1/4 cup/2 fl oz/60 ml tequila or water

2 tablespoons snipped fresh cilantro (fresh coriander/ Chinese parsley)

2 cloves garlic, minced

1 teaspoon ground cumin

1/8 teaspoon salt

Pepper

8 flour tortillas (7 in/18 cm in diameter)

1 tablespoon cooking oil

1 medium onion, halved and thinly sliced

1 medium green, red or yellow bell pepper (capsicum), cut into thin strips

1/2 cup/3 oz/90 g chopped fresh or canned tomatillos or chopped tomatoes

Guacamole (optional)

Sour cream (optional)

Salsa (optional)

Shredded cheddar or Monterey Jack cheese (optional)

157

Chicken strips sautéed with sweet peppers and onions are rolled into a tortilla and served with assorted toppings for an all-in-one meal.

METHOD FOR MAKING CHICKEN FAJITAS

Frying and Sautéing

Preparation time 30 minutes
Marinating time 4 to 24 hours
Cooking time 6 to 8 minutes
Makes 4 servings

STEPS AT A GLANCE	Page
■ Marinating chicken	241
■ Sautéing chicken	130

Place chicken strips in a plastic bag set in a deep bowl. In another bowl stir together ¼ cup/2 fl oz/60 ml oil, lime juice, tequila or water, 1 tablespoon of the cilantro (fresh coriander/Chinese parsley), the garlic, cumin, salt and pepper. Pour over chicken. Seal bag and marinate in the refrigerator for 4 to 24 hours, turning occasionally. Drain chicken from marinade; discard marinade. Set chicken aside.

Wrap tortillas in foil. Heat in a 350°F/180°C/Gas Mark 4 oven for 10 minutes to warm. Meanwhile, preheat a large frying pan over medium-high heat; add 1 tablespoon oil. Cook and stir onion in hot oil for 1½ minutes. Add bell pepper (capsicum) strips; cook and stir about 1½ minutes more, or until vegetables are crisp-tender. Remove vegetables from frying pan.

Add chicken strips to hot pan. (Add more oil, if necessary.) Cook and stir for 2 to 3 minutes, or until tender and no pink remains. Return all vegetables to frying pan. Add tomatillos or tomatoes. Cook and stir for 1 to 2 minutes, or until heated through. Stir in remaining cilantro. To serve, fill tortillas with chicken-vegetable mixture. If desired, top with guacamole, sour cream, salsa and/or cheese.

Sherried Chicken with Orange Sauce

**Another time, try serving this chicken and its citrusy sauce
over curry- or saffron-flavored pasta,
available at some specialty food shops.**

INGREDIENTS

4 boneless, skinless chicken
breast halves (1 lb/500 g total)

1/4 cup/1 oz/30 g all-purpose
(plain) flour

1/2 teaspoon salt

1/4 teaspoon pepper

2 tablespoons olive oil or
cooking oil

1 clove garlic, cut into thin slivers

1/2 cup/4 fl oz/125 ml
cream sherry

1 cup/8 fl oz/250 ml
orange juice

2 tablespoons orange marmalade

1/4 cup/1 oz/30 g sliced almonds,
toasted

Hot cooked rice

For a smart dinner party, present these sherry-laced chicken breasts on parsleyed rice with peas and rolls alongside.

Frying and Sautéing

Preparation time 15 minutes
Cooking time 13 to 17 minutes
Makes 4 servings

Rinse chicken; pat dry. In a large plastic bag combine flour, salt and pepper. Add chicken, 1 piece at a time, shaking bag to coat chicken with flour mixture. In a 10-in/25-cm frying pan heat olive oil or cooking oil over medium heat. Add chicken and cook for 10 to 12 minutes, or until chicken is tender and no longer pink, turning once. Transfer chicken to a serving platter; keep warm.

In the same frying pan cook and stir garlic in the pan drippings for 15 seconds. Carefully add cream sherry. Bring to boiling; boil gently, uncovered, for 1 to 2 minutes, or until reduced by half. Stir in orange juice and orange marmalade. Bring to boiling; boil gently, uncovered, for 2 to 3 minutes, or until slightly thickened. Pour over chicken. Sprinkle with toasted almonds. Serve with rice.

Chicken Diana

If you want to make an impression on your dinner guests,
invite them into the kitchen for the flaming, which makes a good show
but also serves to burn off the alcohol and leave the brandy flavor.

INGREDIENTS

4 boneless, skinless chicken
breast halves (1 lb/500 g total)

2 tablespoons margarine
or butter

2 shallots, finely chopped

2 tablespoons brandy

1/2 cup/4 fl oz/125 ml
chicken stock

2 tablespoons white wine
Worcestershire sauce or plain
Worcestershire sauce

1 teaspoon Dijon-style mustard

2 tablespoons
snipped fresh
parsley

An impressive dish, Chicken Diana merits equally attractive accompaniments. Wide egg noodles with poppy seeds, and asparagus spears sprinkled with red bell pepper work beautifully in a supporting role.

Preparation time 15 minutes
Cooking time 10 to 12 minutes
Makes 4 servings

STEPS AT A GLANCE	Page
■ Skinning and boning	19–21
■ Pounding chicken breasts	46
■ Sautéing chicken	130

Rinse chicken; pat dry. Place each breast half between 2 pieces of plastic wrap. Working from the center to the edges, pound chicken lightly with the flat side of a meat mallet to a 1/4-in/6-mm thickness. Remove plastic wrap.

In a 12-in/30-cm frying pan melt margarine or butter. Add shallots and cook over medium heat until tender. Increase heat to medium-high. Add chicken and cook for 4 to 6 minutes, or until chicken is tender and no pink remains, turning once. Remove from heat. Sprinkle chicken with brandy. Ignite the brandy using a very long match while keeping your hand to the side of the pan. When flame is gone, transfer chicken to a serving platter and keep warm.

In a small mixing bowl stir together chicken stock, Worcestershire sauce and mustard; add to frying pan. Bring to boiling; boil gently about 5 minutes to slightly thicken liquid and reduce it by half. Pour sauce over chicken breasts. Sprinkle with parsley.

Chicken Piccata with Vegetables

A side dish of rich fettuccine Alfredo, or just buttered pasta, would be delicious with this lemony main course. Garnish with lemon and parsley.

INGREDIENTS

4 boneless, skinless chicken breast halves (1 lb/500 g total)

1/4 cup/1 oz/30 g all-purpose (plain) flour

1/8 teaspoon salt

1/8 teaspoon pepper

3 tablespoons margarine or butter

1/4 cup/2 fl oz/60 ml chicken stock

1/4 cup/2 fl oz/60 ml dry white wine, dry white vermouth or chicken stock

1 tablespoon finely shredded lemon peel

2 tablespoons lemon juice

2 tablespoons snipped fresh parsley

2 medium carrots, shredded

2 medium zucchini (courgettes), shredded

1 clove garlic, minced

An update of an Italian classic made with veal, this chicken piccata features the characteristic tart sauce plus a layer of sautéed vegetables.

METHOD FOR MAKING CHICKEN PICCATA WITH VEGETABLES

Preparation time 25 minutes
Cooking time 6 to 8 minutes
Makes 4 servings

Rinse chicken; pat dry. Place each breast half between 2 pieces of plastic wrap. Working from the center to the edges, pound chicken lightly with the flat side of a meat mallet to a ¼-in/6-mm thickness. Remove plastic wrap.

In a shallow dish stir together the flour, salt and pepper. Coat each breast with flour mixture; shake off excess.

In a 12-in/30-cm frying pan melt half of the margarine or butter. Add chicken and cook over medium-high heat for 4 to 6 minutes, or until tender and no pink remains, turning once. Remove chicken from pan; keep warm. In the same pan combine the chicken stock, wine, lemon peel and lemon juice. Bring to boiling; boil until sauce is reduced to about ⅓ cup/2½ fl oz/80 ml. Remove from heat and stir in parsley.

Meanwhile, in a 10-in/25-cm pan melt the remaining margarine or butter. Add the carrots, zucchini (courgettes) and garlic and cook for 2 to 3 minutes, or until carrots are crisp-tender. Transfer vegetables to a serving platter and top with chicken and sauce.

About Phyllo

Delicate, paper-thin and translucent, phyllo dough takes its name from the Greek for "leaf". Stacked layer upon layer to produce a crisp and flaky pastry, phyllo is the basis for many sweet and savory dishes. Traditional favorites are nut-laden and honey-drenched Greek and Turkish pastries, Greek feta-and-spinach triangles and rich German strudels.

In past generations, the art of working and stretching strudel dough until it covered the kitchen table was part of the repertoire of accomplished home bakers. Today, few cooks attempt it. Most recipes that previously called for homemade strudel dough now substitute packaged phyllo dough, which is readily available in supermarkets. The packaged version is considerably more convenient, but still retains the buttery taste and crisp lightness of the homemade version.

To use commercial phyllo dough, defrost it overnight in the refrigerator or use as directed on the package. While preparing the recipe, always keep sheets of phyllo lightly covered with plastic wrap until you use them, so they won't dry out. For the same reason, use a generous amount of melted butter or margarine between layers. Stagger the stacks of phyllo sheets so that the seams aren't all in the one place. When working with large pieces of phyllo dough, a bedsheet makes an unexpected kitchen tool: lightly floured, it will make it much easier to lift the dough and roll it over the filling.

Coat a sautéed chicken breast with duxelles, then wrap in phyllo for a stylish supper.

Chicken with Duxelles Wrapped in Phyllo

The culinary term *duxelles* refers to a cooked mixture of mushrooms and onions.
When working with phyllo dough, keep the extra sheets covered
with a damp towel so they don't dry out.

INGREDIENTS

1 tablespoon cooking oil

4 skinless, boneless chicken breast halves (1 lb/500 g total)

1 tablespoon margarine or butter

8 oz/250 g fresh mushrooms, finely chopped

2 green (spring) onions, finely chopped

1 tablespoon dry white vermouth or dry white wine (optional)

¹/₄ teaspoon salt

¹/₄ teaspoon dried thyme, crushed

Dash pepper

2 tablespoons sour cream

8 sheets phyllo dough, thawed

6 tablespoons margarine or butter, melted

Preparation time 25 minutes
Cooking time 12 to 13 minutes
Baking time 25 minutes
Makes 4 servings

STEPS AT A GLANCE	Page
■ Skinning and boning	19–21
■ Sautéing chicken	130

In a large frying pan heat oil and brown the chicken breasts on both sides. Remove and set aside. In the same pan melt the margarine or butter over medium-high heat. Add mushrooms and onions; cook and stir for about 5 minutes, or until most of the liquid evaporates. Stir in vermouth (if desired), salt, thyme and pepper.

Cook for 2 to 3 minutes more, or until all of the liquid has evaporated. Let cool, then stir in sour cream.

Brush 1 sheet of phyllo with some of the melted margarine or butter. Place another sheet of phyllo on top of the first sheet and brush with margarine or butter. (Keep remaining phyllo covered with a damp towel.) Place a chicken breast in the center of one short end. Spread the top of the chicken with about a fourth of the mushroom mixture. Fold both long sides of phyllo toward the center and brush with margarine or butter. Roll up. Place on a baking sheet and brush top and sides with

margarine or butter. Repeat with remaining phyllo, mushroom mixture, chicken breasts and margarine or butter.

Bake in a preheated 375°F/ 190°C/Gas Mark 4 oven for about 25 minutes, or until phyllo is golden and chicken is tender and no pink remains.

Chicken Breasts with Sauce Suprême

This elegant dish is surprisingly simple to make. Have everything
prepared and measured out in advance so that you can work
quickly, and keep a wooden spoon handy to blend in
all of the densely flavorful bits in the drippings.

INGREDIENTS

2 tablespoons margarine or
butter

4 boneless, skinless chicken breast
halves (1 lb/500 g total)

Salt

Pepper

1/2 cup/1 1/2 oz/45 g sliced fresh
mushrooms

1/4 cup/1 oz/30 g finely chopped
shallots

1/4 cup/2 fl oz/60 ml dry
white wine

1 cup/8 fl oz/250 ml
chicken stock

2 tablespoons all-purpose
(plain) flour

2 teaspoons snipped fresh thyme
or 1/2 teaspoon dried thyme,
crushed

1 bay leaf

3 tablespoons heavy
(double) cream

Salt

White pepper

Hot cooked
linguine or
fettuccine

Frying and Sautéing

Preparation time 20 minutes
Cooking time 15 to 17 minutes
Makes 4 servings

STEPS AT A GLANCE	Page
■ Skinning and boning	19–21
■ Sautéing chicken	130

In a large frying pan melt margarine or butter over medium heat. Add chicken breasts and cook for 10 to 12 minutes, or until chicken is tender and no pink remains, turning once. Sprinkle chicken with salt and pepper. Transfer to a serving platter; keep warm.

In the same pan cook mushrooms and shallots in the chicken drippings for about 3 minutes, or until tender. Spoon over chicken; keep warm. Add white wine to pan, stirring to loosen any crusty browned bits in the bottom of the pan. Stir together chicken stock, flour, thyme and bay leaf. Add to pan. Cook and stir until thickened and bubbly. Cook for 2 minutes more. Stir in cream. Remove bay leaf. Season sauce to taste with salt and white pepper. Serve sauce over chicken and hot cooked pasta.

Serve these golden chicken breasts on a bed of pasta and surround with steamed julienned zucchini and carrots.

Plan a bistro-style menu with these sautéed chicken breast sandwiches and a side of skinny French fries, or pommes frites.

Sautéed Chicken Sandwich with Olives

Turn this recipe into delicious party appetizers
by leaving out the chicken and simply spreading the olive mixture
on slices of sourdough bread that have been brushed with olive oil
and toasted under the broiler.

INGREDIENTS

1/4 cup/1 1/2 oz/45 g chopped pimiento-stuffed olives or Kalamata olives

1 small tomato, chopped

1 tablespoon snipped fresh parsley

2 teaspoons drained capers (optional)

1/2 teaspoon dried Italian seasoning, crushed

1 teaspoon olive oil or cooking oil

4 boneless, skinless chicken breast halves (1 lb/500 g total)

2 tablespoons olive oil or cooking oil

4 lettuce leaves

4 slices sourdough bread, toasted

Preparation time 20 minutes
Cooking time 4 to 6 minutes
Makes 4 servings

In a small mixing bowl stir together olives, tomato, parsley, capers (if desired), Italian seasoning and the 1 teaspoon olive oil or cooking oil. Set aside.

Place each breast half between 2 pieces of plastic wrap. Working from the center to the edges, pound chicken lightly with the flat side of a meat mallet to a 1/4-in/6-mm thickness. Remove plastic wrap.

In a large frying pan cook chicken in the 2 tablespoons olive oil or cooking oil over medium-high heat for 4 to 6 minutes, or until tender and no pink remains, turning once. Remove from pan.

To serve, place lettuce leaves on toasted sourdough bread. Top with chicken breasts and olive mixture.

Rhineland Chicken Burgers

These soft patties will be easier to shape if you wet your hands;
the patties will firm up as they cook. You can grind the chicken yourself,
or you may find it already prepared and packaged in supermarket meat departments.

INGREDIENTS

1 beaten egg

2 tablespoons milk

1/4 cup/1 oz/30 g fine dry
breadcrumbs

1/4 cup/1 oz/30 g finely chopped
green (spring) onion

2 tablespoons snipped
fresh parsley

1 teaspoon anchovy paste

1 teaspoon finely shredded
lemon peel

1/4 teaspoon salt

1/4 teaspoon pepper

1 lb/500 g ground
(minced) chicken

2 tablespoons
margarine or butter

Preparation time 15 minutes
Cooking time 8 to 12 minutes
Makes 4 servings

STEPS AT A GLANCE   Page

■ Sautéing chicken pieces   130

In a mixing bowl stir together egg, milk, breadcrumbs, green (spring) onion, parsley, anchovy paste, lemon peel, salt and pepper. Add chicken and mix well. (Mixture will be soft.) Shape chicken mixture into four ³/4-in/2-cm thick patties.

In a large frying pan melt the margarine or butter. Add chicken patties and cook over medium heat for 8 to 12 minutes, or until no pink remains, turning once. Or, to broil (grill), preheat broiler and place patties on the unheated rack of a broiler pan. Broil 3 to 4 inches from the heat for 10 to 12 minutes, turning once.

Complement the German theme by serving these patties with toasted dark bread and cooked red potatoes and onions dressed in a vinaigrette made with coarse-grain mustard.

STIR-FRYING

Stir-Frying Chicken

Like sautéing, stir-frying is a quick-cooking method using an open pan and a small amount of fat. There are some differences, however. Sautéing, a classic French technique, involves large pieces of meat, such as boneless chicken breasts, cooked in a straight-sided sauté pan or frying pan. Stir-frying, an Asian method, requires all the ingredients to be in small, uniform pieces; these are tossed until done in a hot wok, a pan with deep, flared sides.

If you have ever seen a stir-fry chef in action in a restaurant, you know how fast-paced this technique can be. There isn't time to stop between steps to slice a mushroom or mix a marinade. Preparing ahead makes it all go smoothly, from adding oil to blending the sauce. Before you begin cooking, measure, mix, cut up and slice all the ingredients and arrange them in bowls near the stove so they are within easy reach.

Setting yourself up with the right utensils is not very expensive. Woks and other specialty equipment for stir-frying are available from well-stocked kitchenware stores, by mail order from catalogs or at Asian markets.

BASIC TOOLS FOR STIR-FRYING

Stir-frying uses some specialized equipment, including a spatula–stirrer and the deep, flare-sided pan known as a wok, but you can make do with a large frying pan and a wooden spoon.

wok

small bowls and cutting board

wok spatula

wooden spoon

measuring spoon

chef's knife

185

Stir-Frying

Similarly sized pieces will cook evenly and quickly.

STEP 1

Cutting Chicken Cubes or Strips
Depending on what the recipe calls for, cut boneless chicken breasts or thighs into square pieces or thin strips of approximately the same size.

Cut all vegetables for stir-frying into small, uniform pieces.

STEP 2

Cutting Bell Peppers (Capsicums) into Strips
With a medium knife, cut the bell pepper in half and remove the stem, ribs and seeds. Cut each half into uniform lengthwise strips, then cut the strips in half crosswise to make them bite-sized.

If using a large frying pan rather than a wok, add the oil and tilt the pan to make sure the oil coats the bottom and extends slightly up the sides.

STEP 3

Adding Oil to the Wok

Starting at the top of the pan, swirl 1 tablespoon of oil around the sides of the wok. This allows the oil to flow down the pan sides and coat them completely.

First, stir-fry vegetables that need a longer cooking time, such as carrots, onions and beans, then add ones that don't need as much time.

STEP 4

Stir-Frying

With a spatula or long-handled wooden spoon, use a folding motion to gently lift and turn the pieces of food so that each is exposed to the hot, oil-coated cooking surface.

Stir-Frying

If the sauce contains cornstarch (cornflour), stir it again before adding it to the wok.

STEP 5

Stirring in Sauce

When the chicken pieces are no longer pink, push them away from the center of the wok. Pour in the sauce and cook, stirring, until the liquid thickens and bubbles. Return vegetables to pan.

Stir-fried chicken and vegetables cooked in a small amount of fat make a light and healthy meal. The recipe for this Bell Pepper Stir-fry is on page 214.

Serve this traditional Chinese stir-fry family-style over noodles on a platter, with big chopsticks (or tongs) for serving.

Chicken Cantonese

This chicken dish is loaded with traditional Cantonese ingredients
such as rice wine, sesame oil and ginger.
It is just as tasty served over rice instead of the egg noodles.

INGREDIENTS

2 tablespoons soy sauce

1 tablespoon rice wine or
chicken stock

2 teaspoons cornstarch
(cornflour)

12 oz/375 g boneless, skinless
chicken breast halves, cut into
thin bite-sized strips

1 cup/8 fl oz/250 ml
chicken stock

1 tablespoon cornstarch
(cornflour)

6 oz/185 g dried Chinese egg
noodles or regular fine egg
noodles

1 teaspoon toasted sesame oil

1 tablespoon cooking oil

2 cloves garlic, minced

2 teaspoons grated ginger root

2 oz/60 g thinly bias-sliced carrot

2 oz/60 g thinly bias-sliced celery

5 oz/155 g thinly sliced
red and/or green bell pepper
(capsicum)

2½ oz/75 g chopped onion

3 oz/90 g sliced fresh
mushrooms

⅓ cup/2 oz/60 g coarsely
chopped almonds

Stir-Frying

METHOD FOR MAKING CHICKEN CANTONESE

Preparation time 20 minutes
Marinating time 30 minutes
Cooking time 12 to 14 minutes
Makes 4 servings

In a medium mixing bowl stir together soy sauce, rice wine or chicken stock and 2 teaspoons cornstarch (cornflour). Stir in chicken and let stand at room temperature for 30 minutes. Do not drain.

Meanwhile, in a small bowl stir together 1 cup/8 fl oz/ 250 ml chicken stock and 1 tablespoon cornstarch. Set aside. Cook egg noodles according to package directions; drain noodles then return to pan. Stir in sesame oil. Keep warm.

Pour cooking oil into a wok or large frying pan. (Add more oil during cooking if food starts to stick.) Preheat over medium-high heat. Stir-fry garlic and ginger root in hot oil for 15 seconds. Add carrot; stir-fry for 1 minute. Add celery and stir-fry for 1 minute. Add bell pepper and onion; stir-fry for 1 minute. Add mushrooms; stir-fry for 1 minute more, or till vegetables are crisp-tender. Remove all vegetables from wok

Add almonds to hot wok; stir-fry for 2 to 3 minutes, or until toasted. Remove from wok. Add undrained chicken to hot wok; stir-fry for 3 to 4 minutes, or until tender and no pink remains. Push chicken away from center of wok. Stir chicken stock-cornstarch mixture; add to center of wok. Cook and stir until thickened and bubbly. Return vegetables and almonds to wok. Stir all ingredients together to coat with sauce. Cook and stir about 1 minute more, or until heated through. Serve over noodles.

Bias-Slicing Carrots
Hold a chef's knife at a 45-degree angle to the peeled carrot and make the first cut. Make evenly spaced cuts at the same angle for the entire length of the carrot.

Grating Ginger
Cut a slice off of one edge of an unpeeled piece of ginger root to remove the woody end. Hold the ginger root at a 45-degree angle to a ginger grater or fine grater and rub across the grating surface.

Crystal Chicken with Broccoli

To vary the colors and flavors of this dish, use 3 cups mixed vegetables in place of the broccoli. Bell peppers (capsicums), carrots and asparagus are good choices.

INGREDIENTS

3/4 cup/4 oz/125 g all-purpose (plain) flour

1/4 teaspoon baking powder

3/4 cup/6 fl oz/180 ml water

2 tablespoons soy sauce

2 cloves garlic, flattened

1/4 cup/3 fl oz/90 ml honey

2 tablespoons soy sauce

2 tablespoons cider vinegar

2 tablespoons molasses

2 tablespoons water

2 tablespoons dry sherry

2 cloves garlic, minced

2 teaspoons cornstarch (cornflour)

12 oz/375 g boneless, skinless chicken breast halves

Cooking oil for deep-fat frying

1 tablespoon cooking oil

6 oz/185 g broccoli florets

Stir-fried nuggets of chicken combine with broccoli florets for this homemade version of a favorite from Chinese restaurants.

Preparation time 40 minutes
Cooking time 10 to 12 minutes
Makes 4 servings

In a medium mixing bowl stir together flour, baking powder, ¾ cup/6 fl oz/190 ml water, 2 tablespoons soy sauce, and flattened garlic; let stand for 15 minutes. Remove and discard the garlic.

Meanwhile, in a small mixing bowl combine the honey, 2 tablespoons soy sauce, vinegar molasses, 2 tablespoons water, dry sherry, minced garlic and cornstarch (cornflour); set aside. Rinse chicken; pat dry. Cut chicken into 1½- x ½-in/4-cm x 12-mm strips. Add to flour batter.

In a wok or 2 qt/2 l saucepan heat 2 in/5 cm of oil to 365°F/185°C. Remove chicken from flour batter, allowing excess to drain off. Fry chicken strips, a few pieces at a time, in hot oil for 30 to 60 seconds, or until golden. Drain on paper towels.

Pour 1 tablespoon cooking oil into a large frying pan. (Add more oil as necessary during cooking.) Preheat over medium-high heat. Add the broccoli and stir-fry for 4 to 5 minutes, or until crisp-tender. Arrange broccoli around the edge of a serving platter; keep warm.

Stir honey–soy mixture; add to the frying pan. Cook and stir until thickened and bubbly. Cook and stir for 1 minute more. Return cooked chicken to pan; heat through. Pour chicken and sauce into center of broccoli-lined serving platter.

Stir-Frying

Trimming Broccoli Florets
Cut away the florets from the stalk with a paring knife.
Halve large pieces so all of the florets are similar in size.

Deep-Frying Chicken
Pour oil into a wok or saucepan; heat to 365°F/185°C
(test with a deep-fat thermometer). Drain chicken of
excess batter and fry, a few pieces at a time, until golden.
Lift out with a slotted spoon; drain on paper towels.

Look for cilantro (fresh coriander/
Chinese parsley) and fish sauce, the
signature flavors in this dish, in a
well-stocked supermarket or
Asian grocer.

Thai-Style Chicken and Spinach

Two special ingredients give this dish its unique flavor.
Thai fish sauce, or *nam pla*, is a fermented liquid with a rich flavor.
Cilantro is the leaf of the coriander plant. If you prefer a milder dish,
you can substitute peanut oil for the hot chili oil.

INGREDIENTS

1/4 cup/2 fl oz/60 g chicken stock

1 tablespoon fish sauce or
2 teaspoons soy sauce

1 tablespoon cornstarch
(cornflour)

2 tablespoons snipped fresh
cilantro (fresh coriander/
Chinese parsley)

12 oz/375 g boneless,
skinless chicken thighs, cut into
1-in/2.5-cm pieces

1 tablespoon hot chili oil

2 10-oz bags/1 1/4 lb/625 g
spinach leaves, washed
and trimmed

3 cloves garlic, minced

1/4 cup/2 oz/60 g chopped
peanuts

Preparation time 20 minutes
Cooking time 8 to 10 minutes
Makes 4 servings

In a small bowl combine chicken stock, fish sauce or soy sauce and cornstarch (cornflour); set aside.

In a large mixing bowl toss cilantro (fresh coriander/Chinese parsley) with chicken. Pour hot chili oil into a wok or large frying pan. Preheat over medium-high heat. Stir-fry chicken for 2 to 3 minutes, or until no pink remains. Remove chicken from wok.

Add spinach and garlic to wok; toss to mix. Return chicken to the wok. Reduce heat to medium-low; cover and cook for 3 minutes. Push chicken and vegetables away from center of wok to the sides of the pan.

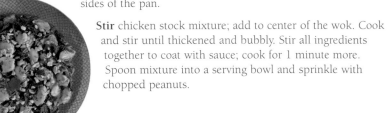

Stir chicken stock mixture; add to center of the wok. Cook and stir until thickened and bubbly. Stir all ingredients together to coat with sauce; cook for 1 minute more. Spoon mixture into a serving bowl and sprinkle with chopped peanuts.

About Peanuts

Peanuts are not true nuts at all, but the seeds of an annual legume that grows to 6–24 in/15–60 cm. The seeds grow on long tendrils just below the ground, which is why they are sometimes called groundnuts. Peanuts are unknown in the wild, but evidence from Inca tombs indicates that they originated and were first cultivated in South America. In the 16th century, Portuguese slave traders carried the nuts from Brazil to West Africa, from where they were introduced to the United States. Today peanuts are an important world crop. Some countries, such as the United States, grow peanuts mainly for use as whole nuts and peanut butter; other countries, such as India and China, for oil.

The nuts have many uses around the world. In Asia, they are used in soups, stews, curries and satays. In Africa, roasted peanut meal forms the basis of a common dish called groundnut chop or stew. In North America and Europe they are mostly used in sweet dishes, candy, cookies and cakes. They are also processed into vegetarian products such as nut meats. Peanut oil is used as a cooking oil, in margarine and in canning fish. Oilcakes, the residue left after oil extraction, are used for animal feed.

In most recipes, peanuts are first roasted to remove the unpleasant raw taste. (Unless labeled as raw, most shop-bought peanuts will already have been roasted.) Roast them in a 240°F/115°C /Gas Mark 1 oven until the nuts are dry, the flesh pale brown and the skins brittle. Store peanuts in an airtight container in a cool place or in the refrigerator, or freeze them for long storage periods.

Sesame Chicken with Vegetables

To deep-fry the chicken pieces, follow the procedure shown on page 197.
When mixing the fried pieces with the sauce at the end,
don't cook them too long or the coating may become soggy.

INGREDIENTS

SAUCE

1/2 cup/4 fl oz/125 ml
chicken stock

2 tablespoons soy sauce

1 tablespoon toasted sesame oil

4 cloves garlic, minced

2 to 3 teaspoons grated
ginger root

2 teaspoons cornstarch
(cornflour)

1 teaspoon sugar

CHICKEN

1/2 cup/2 oz/60 g all-purpose
(plain) flour

2 tablespoons sesame seeds

1/2 teaspoon salt

1/4 teaspoon ground red
(cayenne) pepper

1 beaten egg

1/4 cup/2 fl oz/60 ml milk

Cooking oil for deep-fat frying

1 lb/500 g boneless, skinless
chicken thighs, cut into
3/4-in/2-cm pieces

VEGETABLES

1 tablespoon cooking oil

2 zucchini (courgettes), cut
into thin, bite-sized strips

1 green bell pepper (capsicum),
cut into thin, bite-sized strips

6 green (spring) onions,
bias-sliced into 1/2-in/12-mm
pieces

Arrange stir-fried chicken and
vegetables around a mound of hot
cooked rice that has been molded
in a bowl and inverted onto the
platter. Garnish with lemon,
sesame seeds and green
(spring) onion tops.

Preparation time 20 minutes
Cooking time about 25 minutes
Makes 6 servings

For sauce, in a small bowl stir together chicken stock, soy sauce, sesame oil, garlic, ginger root, cornstarch (cornflour) and sugar. Set aside.

For chicken, in a large mixing bowl combine flour, sesame seeds, salt and ground red (cayenne) pepper. In a small mixing bowl combine egg and milk. Add to dry ingredients and beat until smooth. In a wok or 2 qt/2 l saucepan heat 1¹/₄ in/3 cm cooking oil to 365°F/185°C. Dip chicken, 1 piece at a time, into the coating, then add to hot oil. Fry chicken, a few pieces at a time, about 4 minutes, or until golden. Using a slotted spoon, remove chicken from oil. Drain on paper towels. Keep warm in a preheated 300°F/150°C /Gas Mark 2 oven while stir-frying vegetables.

For vegetables, pour cooking oil into a large frying pan. (Add more oil as necessary during cooking.) Preheat over medium-high heat. Stir-fry zucchini (courgettes), green bell pepper (capsicum), and green (spring) onions for 3 minutes, or until crisp-tender. Push vegetables from the center of the frying pan. Stir sauce; add to the pan. Cook and stir until thickened and bubbly. Cook for 1 minute more. Return the cooked chicken to the pan. Stir all ingredients together to coat with sauce. Serve immediately.

Warm Thai Chicken Salad

Warm salads are a feature of Thai cooking. This one combines sweet and tart flavors with a touch of chili.

INGREDIENTS

CHICKEN AND MARINADE

3 boneless, skinless chicken breast fillets (1¹/₂ lb/750 g total)

¹/₄ cup/2 fl oz/60 ml fresh lemon juice

¹/₄ teaspoon salt

2 cloves garlic, minced

1 tablespoon brown sugar

2 tablespoons finely chopped cilantro (fresh coriander/ Chinese parsley)

DRESSING

1 small red chili, finely chopped

1 clove garlic, finely chopped

3 tablespoons extra virgin olive oil

1 tablespoon balsamic vinegar

Juice of 2 limes

1 teaspoon sweet chili sauce

SALAD

1 bunch/14 oz/440 g mizuna lettuce

1 red bell pepper (capsicum), thinly sliced

2 carrots, cut into thin strips

1 cucumber, cut into thin strips

6 green (spring) onions, sliced

1 cup/1 oz/30 g loosely packed cilantro (fresh coriander/ Chinese parsley) sprigs

1 cup/1 oz/30 g shredded purple basil

3 tablespoons toasted sesame oil

3 tablespoons toasted sesame seeds

This colorful salad with its piquant sweet-and-sour style dressing makes a delightful light lunch on a summer day.

Preparation time 20 minutes
Cooking time 5 minutes
Marinating time 4–12 hours
Makes 6 small servings

Flatten the chicken fillets slightly with the flat side of a meat mallet. Cut each lengthwise into 4 strips. Combine all of the marinade ingredients in a shallow glass or ceramic bowl and mix well. Add the chicken and toss to coat. Cover with plastic wrap and set aside in the refrigerator overnight or for several hours.

For the dressing, combine all dressing ingredients in a small bowl and whisk until well combined.

Combine the mizuna, red bell pepper (capsicum), carrot, cucumber, green (spring) onion, cilantro (fresh coriander/Chinese parsley) and basil. Divide among 6 individual serving plates.

Heat the sesame oil in a wok or frying pan until smoking. Stir-fry the chicken for about 3 minutes, or until no pink remains. Divide the chicken among the serving plates. Drizzle on the dressing and sprinkle with the toasted sesame seeds. Serve immediately, while the chicken is still warm.

Sweet and Sour Chicken

We used cracker crumbs instead of the customary batter to coat the chicken pieces
for this perennial favorite. This not only decreases the preparation time,
it reduces the fat content of the finished dish as well.

INGREDIENTS

16 oz/1 lb/500 g can pineapple chunks (including juice)

1/4 cup/2 fl oz/60 ml ketchup (tomato sauce)

1 tablespoon cornstarch (cornflour)

2 tablespoons red wine vinegar

2 tablespoons water

4 teaspoons sugar

1 beaten egg

1 tablespoon cornstarch (cornflour)

12 oz/375 g boneless, skinless chicken breast halves, cut into 1-in/2.5-cm cubes

3/4 cup/2 oz/60 g finely crushed saltine (plain savory) crackers

1 tablespoon cooking oil

1 green bell pepper (capsicum), cut into 1/2-in/12-mm pieces

1 red bell pepper (capsicum), cut into 1/2-in/12-mm pieces

4 green (spring) onions, bias-sliced into 1 1/2-in/4-cm pieces

Hot cooked rice (optional)

A pretty Oriental platter complements the hues of this Chinese classic.

Preparation time 20 minutes
Cooking time 12 to 14 minutes
Makes 4 servings

STEPS AT A GLANCE   Page

■ Skinning and boning   19–21
■ Stir-frying chicken   186–188

Drain pineapple, reserving ¾ cup/6 fl oz/180 ml juice. In a small bowl stir together the reserved pineapple juice, the ketchup (tomato sauce), 1 tablespoon cornstarch (cornflour), vinegar, water and sugar. Set aside.

In a medium mixing bowl stir together egg and 1 tablespoon cornstarch (cornflour) until smooth. Add chicken pieces and stir to coat chicken with egg mixture. Pour cracker crumbs into a shallow dish. Roll chicken pieces in cracker crumbs to coat evenly.

Preheat oil over medium-high heat in a wok or large frying pan. Add half of the chicken and stir-fry about 3 minutes, or until no pink remains. Remove chicken from wok and keep warm. Repeat with remaining chicken.

Add bell pepper (capsicum) and green (spring) onion to wok; stir-fry for 2 to 3 minutes, or until crisp-tender. Remove vegetables from wok.

Stir pineapple juice mixture; add to wok. Cook and stir until thickened and bubbly. Cook and stir for 2 minutes more. Return chicken, vegetables and pineapple chunks to wok. Stir all ingredients together to coat with sauce. Cook and stir about 1 minute more, or until heated through. If desired, serve with rice.

Stir-Fried Chicken Thighs with Fresh Asparagus

While the chicken is marinating, prepare the sauce and vegetables. After cleaning the asparagus, hold each spear in one hand and bend it gently until the end snaps off; discard ends.

INGREDIENTS

1 lightly beaten egg white

1 tablespoon cornstarch (cornflour)

1 tablespoon dry white wine

1 clove garlic, minced

1/4 teaspoon salt

1/4 teaspoon white pepper

1 lb/500 g boneless, skinless chicken thighs, cut into thin, bite-sized strips

2 tablespoons chili sauce

2 tablespoons soy sauce

1 tablespoon wine vinegar

1 to 1 1/2 teaspoons chili oil

1 tablespoon cooking oil

1 lb/500 g asparagus spears, bias-sliced into 2-in/5-cm pieces

1 red bell pepper (capsicum), cut into bite-sized strips

4 green (spring) onions, bias-sliced into 1-in/2.5-cm pieces

A bowl of rice with a colorful blend of chicken and vegetables makes a quick, simple, satisfying meal.

Stir-Frying

Preparation time 20 minutes
Marinating time 20 to 30 minutes
Cooking time 12 to 14 minutes
Makes 4 servings

In a medium mixing bowl stir together the egg white, cornstarch (cornflour), wine, garlic, salt and white pepper. Stir in the chicken strips. Cover and let stand at room temperature for 20 to 30 minutes. Do not drain. Meanwhile, in a small bowl stir together chili sauce, soy sauce, wine vinegar and chili oil. Set aside.

Pour cooking oil into a wok or large frying pan. (Add more oil as necessary during cooking.) Preheat over medium-high heat. Stir-fry half of the asparagus, bell pepper (capsicum), and green (spring) onion for 3 to 4 minutes, or until crisp-tender. Remove from wok. Repeat with the remaining vegetables.

Add undrained chicken strips to hot wok. Stir-fry for 3 to 4 minutes, or until no pink remains. Return cooked vegetables to wok. Stir chili sauce mixture; stir into chicken and vegetables. Cover wok and cook about 1 minute more, or until heated through.

Bell Pepper Stir-Fry

**Here's a stir-fry with Mediterranean influences.
The capers give this ultra-quick dish an unexpected tang.**

INGREDIENTS

1 cup/8 fl oz/250 ml
chicken stock

2 tablespoons all-purpose
(plain) flour

2 tablespoons tomato paste

1/2 teaspoon paprika

1/4 teaspoon salt

1/4 teaspoon pepper

1 tablespoon cooking oil

1 large onion, cut into
thin wedges

1 cup/3 oz/90 g sliced
fresh mushrooms

1 medium green bell pepper
(capsicum), cut into thin,
bite-sized strips

1 medium red bell pepper
(capsicum), cut into thin,
bite-sized strips

12 oz/375 g boneless,
skinless chicken thighs, cut into
bite-sized strips

1 tablespoon
drained capers
or 2 tablespoons
chopped dill pickle
(optional)

Hot cooked pasta
or rice

*Corkscrew pasta, or
rotelle, makes the perfect
base for a stir-fry with
European flavors.*

METHOD FOR MAKING BELL PEPPER STIR-FRY

Preparation time 20 minutes
Marinating time 8 to 10 minutes
Makes 4 servings

In a small bowl stir together the chicken stock, flour, tomato paste, paprika, salt and pepper. Set aside.

Pour cooking oil into a wok or large frying pan. (Add more oil as necessary during cooking.) Preheat over medium-high heat. Stir-fry onion for 1½ minutes. Add mushrooms; stir-fry for 1 to 2 minutes, or until tender. Remove onion and mushrooms from wok.

Add green and red bell pepper (capsicum); stir-fry for about 1½ minutes, or until pepper is crisp-tender. Remove from wok. Add chicken strips; stir-fry for 2 to 3 minutes, or until no pink remains. Push chicken from center of wok. Stir chicken stock mixture; add sauce to the center of the wok. Cook and stir until thickened and bubbly.

Return vegetables to wok. If desired, add capers or dill pickle. Stir all ingredients together to coat with sauce. Cook and stir about 1 minute more, or until heated through. Serve over pasta or rice.

Ginger Chicken with Peas and Shiitakes

Although you'll pay more for shiitake mushrooms, their flavor
is woodier and richer than that of white mushrooms and well worth the extra expense.
Many supermarkets carry a wide selection of fresh mushrooms.

INGREDIENTS

1 cup/5 oz/155 g snow peas
(mangetout), tips and strings
removed

1 cup/5 oz/155 g loose-pack
frozen peas

3/4 cup/6 fl oz/180 ml
half-and-half (half cream) or
light (single) cream

2 teaspoons cornstarch
(cornflour)

1/2 teaspoon salt

1/8 teaspoon pepper

1 tablespoon cooking oil

2 teaspoons grated fresh
ginger root

8 oz/250 g fresh shiitake
mushrooms or other
mushrooms, stems
removed and sliced

12 oz/375 g boneless,
skinless chicken breast
halves, cut into thin
bite-sized strips

1/4 cup/1/2 oz/15 g snipped
fresh parsley

Fresh shiitake mushrooms, two types of peas and a cream sauce give this stir-fry a delicious difference. Serve over barley or rice.

Preparation time 20 minutes
Marinating time 10 to 12 minutes
Makes 4 servings

In a medium saucepan cook snow peas (mangetout) and green peas in boiling water for 1 minute, or until snow peas are crisp-tender. Drain and set aside.

In a bowl stir together half-and-half (half cream) or light (single) cream, cornstarch (cornflour), salt and pepper. Set aside.

Pour oil into a wok or large frying pan. (Add more oil as necessary during cooking.) Preheat over medium-high heat. Stir-fry ginger root in hot oil for 30 seconds. Add mushrooms; stir-fry for about 2 minutes, or until tender. Remove vegetables from wok.

Add chicken strips to hot wok. Stir-fry for 3 to 4 minutes, or until no pink remains. Push chicken from center of wok. Stir half-and-half mixture; add to the center of wok. Cook and stir until thickened and bubbly. Return cooked vegetables and parsley to wok. Stir all ingredients together to coat with sauce. Cook and stir for 1 minute more, or until heated through. Sprinkle with parsley.

Chicken with Artichokes

When they are in season, you can replace the frozen or canned artichokes with small, fresh artichokes that have been trimmed of their outer leaves, thorny tops and fuzzy chokes.

INGREDIENTS

1/2 cup/4 fl oz/125 ml chicken stock

1 tablespoon white wine Worcestershire sauce

1 tablespoon snipped fresh oregano or 1 teaspoon dried oregano, crushed

2 teaspoons snipped fresh thyme or 1/2 teaspoon dried thyme, crushed

2 teaspoons cornstarch (cornflour)

1/8 teaspoon crushed red (cayenne) pepper

3 slices bacon, cut into 1/2-in/12-mm pieces

1 tablespoon cooking oil

2 cloves garlic, minced

1 red bell pepper (capsicum), cut into 3/4-in/2-cm pieces

1 medium onion, thinly sliced and separated into rings

12 oz/375 g boneless, skinless chicken breast halves or thighs, cut into bite-sized pieces

9-oz package frozen artichoke hearts, thawed, or 9 oz/280 g canned

*Fresh herbal
flavors and chunky
vegetables give this
stir-fry a decidedly
Mediterranean character.
Try it with penne pasta
or macaroni.*

Preparation time 20 minutes
Marinating time 10 to 12 minutes
Makes 4 servings

In a small bowl, stir together chicken stock, Worcestershire sauce, oregano, thyme, cornstarch (cornflour) and crushed red (cayenne) pepper. Set aside.

In a wok or large frying pan cook the bacon until crisp; drain on paper towels. Drain fat. Wipe wok or frying pan clean with paper towels. Pour cooking oil into wok. Preheat over medium-high heat. Stir-fry garlic in hot oil for 15 seconds. Add bell pepper and onion; stir-fry for 2 minutes, or until crisp-tender. Remove from wok.

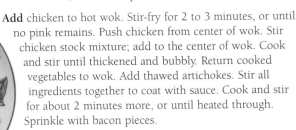

Add chicken to hot wok. Stir-fry for 2 to 3 minutes, or until no pink remains. Push chicken from center of wok. Stir chicken stock mixture; add to the center of wok. Cook and stir until thickened and bubbly. Return cooked vegetables to wok. Add thawed artichokes. Stir all ingredients together to coat with sauce. Cook and stir for about 2 minutes more, or until heated through. Sprinkle with bacon pieces.

About Artichokes

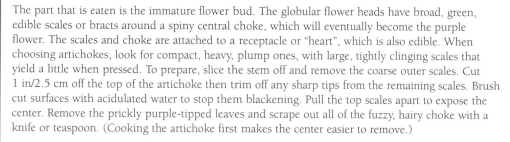

A perennial, thistlelike plant growing 32–72 in/80–180 cm in height, artichokes originated in the Mediterranean region. They are no longer found wild, but have been cultivated for thousands of years, and were known as food plants to the ancient Greeks and Romans. Despite the name, they are not related to Jerusalem artichokes, an edible tuber similar in appearance and flavor to the potato.

The part that is eaten is the immature flower bud. The globular flower heads have broad, green, edible scales or bracts around a spiny central choke, which will eventually become the purple flower. The scales and choke are attached to a receptacle or "heart", which is also edible. When choosing artichokes, look for compact, heavy, plump ones, with large, tightly clinging scales that yield a little when pressed. To prepare, slice the stem off and remove the coarse outer scales. Cut 1 in/2.5 cm off the top of the artichoke then trim off any sharp tips from the remaining scales. Brush cut surfaces with acidulated water to stop them blackening. Pull the top scales apart to expose the center. Remove the prickly purple-tipped leaves and scrape out all of the fuzzy, hairy choke with a knife or teaspoon. (Cooking the artichoke first makes the center easier to remove.)

Artichokes may be boiled or steamed; classic accompaniments are vinaigrette or hollandaise sauce. They can also be stuffed and baked. Artichoke hearts are readily available canned, and make robust additions to pasta sauces, pizzas and salads.

BRAISING

Braising Chicken

Braising combines two cooking techniques. First the meat is sautéed in a little butter or oil to develop its color and flavor, then it is slowly cooked in a small amount of liquid—just enough to keep it succulent and to later form the basis of a pan sauce—in a covered pan, either on top of the stove or in the oven.

Stewing is similar to braising, although the meat is not always browned first and much more cooking liquid is used. Stewing meat is usually cut into smaller pieces than meat for braising.

Although the cooking time is long compared to rapid methods such as stir-fries or sautés, braising and stewing make few demands on the cook other than to check the heat occasionally or to see if the cooking liquid needs replenishing. In fact, both braises and stews are ideal fare for entertaining because they keep well and actually improve in flavor by sitting. Another attraction is that braises may be almost complete meals. Most have vegetables cooked along with the meat. All that is needed are accompaniments such as noodles, rice or potatoes to soak up the sauce. A braise also can be a wonderful low-fat choice, as the chicken can be skinned without the risk of it drying out

in cooking. When browning chicken (the first step in braising), don't crowd the pieces or they won't develop good color; see pages 129–131 for more information on proper sautéing technique. Use a heavy pan with a lid. You can brown the chicken in one pan and then simmer it in another, but you will lose all the delicious bits that stick to the bottom of the pan and add so much flavor to any sauce. For braises and stews that finish cooking in the oven, be sure that the pan is safe for both stovetop and oven use. A Dutch oven or other heavy pan with a tight-fitting lid holds in the juices best.

BASIC TOOLS FOR BRAISING

Braised or stewed chicken will stay moist and juicy if
simmered in a heavy frying pan with a snug-fitting lid.
Use tongs to move chicken pieces and a measuring
cup for adding liquid to the pan.

large frying
pan and lid

measuring
cup

tongs

The bits left over from browning the chicken add richness to the cooking liquid.

STEP 1

Browning Chicken

Add oil to the pan and brown the chicken breast halves or other chicken pieces over medium heat. Using tongs, turn the pieces and brown them on the other side. Remove from the pan.

A braise uses more liquid than a sauté, and a stew uses more liquid still.

STEP 2

Adding Liquid to the Pan

After any other ingredients have been briefly sautéed, return the chicken to the pan and pour in the cooking liquid so that it is evenly distributed around the food.

At a simmer, bubbles will form slowly and break just below the surface.

STEP 3

Simmering the Ingredients

Bring the liquid to a boil, then reduce heat. Cover and simmer until the chicken is tender and cooked through. Sometimes the final simmering is done in the oven. If so, use a pan with heatproof handles and lid. Or, wrap the lid and handles with heavy-duty foil.

Succulent, flavorful Braised Chicken with Apple–Cream Sauce (see page 257) epitomizes the delicious art of braising.

In France, this rich, pungent dish is usually served with parsleyed potatoes to soak up some of its delicious gravy.

Hearty Coq au Vin

This traditional French braise may be made with white wine,
but a deep red-wine flavor has become its hallmark.
It is an ideal way to use the last cupful of an unfinished bottle.

INGREDIENTS

CROUTONS

4 slices French bread

4 teaspoons olive oil

1 clove garlic, halved

COQ AU VIN

2 to 2½ lb/1 to 1.25 kg meaty chicken pieces (breasts, thighs and drumsticks)

1 tablespoon margarine or butter

1 tablespoon cooking oil

Salt

Pepper

1½ cups/4½ oz/140 g fresh mushrooms, cut into quarters

12 pearl or pickling onions, peeled

2 slices bacon, cut up

2 cloves garlic, minced

2 tablespoons all-purpose (plain) flour

1 cup/8 fl oz/250 ml chicken stock

1 cup/8 fl oz/250 ml dry red wine

2 tablespoons tomato paste

1 tomato, peeled, seeded and chopped

1 tablespoon snipped fresh parsley

1 tablespoon snipped fresh tarragon or 1 teaspoon dried tarragon, crushed

1 bay leaf

2 tablespoons snipped fresh parsley

Preparation time 25 minutes
Baking time 1 hour
Makes 4 servings

STEPS AT A GLANCE	Page
■ Making croutons	233
■ Braising chicken	228

For croutons, lightly brush both sides of French bread slices with olive oil. Rub with cut side of garlic clove. Cut bread slices into 3/4- to 1-in/2- to 2.5-cm pieces. Place the bread cubes in a shallow baking pan. Bake in a preheated 300°F/150°C/Gas Mark 2 oven for about 15 minutes or until crisp, stirring once. Set 1 cup of the croutons aside until serving time. Cover and store remaining croutons for another use.

For coq au vin, skin chicken, if desired. Rinse chicken; pat dry. In a Dutch oven or flameproof casserole dish brown chicken pieces on all sides in hot margarine or butter and oil. Remove chicken from Dutch oven; sprinkle with salt and pepper.

In the same Dutch oven cook mushrooms, onions, bacon and garlic until tender. Drain off fat, reserving 2 tablespoons in Dutch oven. Stir flour into reserved fat and cook for 1 minute. Add chicken stock, wine, tomato paste, chopped tomato, 1 tablespoon parsley, tarragon and bay leaf. Return chicken pieces to Dutch oven; bring to boiling. Cover and bake in a preheated 350°F/180°C/Gas Mark 4 oven for 45 minutes. Remove bay leaf. If necessary, skim off excess fat. Top each serving with some of the croutons and 2 tablespoons snipped parsley.

STEP I

Rubbing Bread with Garlic
Slice French bread 1 in/2.5 cm thick. Brush the slices with olive oil. Halve a clove of garlic and rub it across both sides of the bread slices.

STEP 2

Cutting Croutons
Cut the coated bread slices in ³/₄- to 1-in/2- to 2.5-cm strips with a serrated knife; don't separate the strips. Then hold the knife crosswise to the strips and slice again, creating ³/₄- to 1-in/2- to 2.5-cm cubes.

Alsatian-Style Chicken and Dumplings

If you substitute apple juice or cider for the wine, use one tablespoon of brown sugar
rather than two, since the cider is already sweetened.

INGREDIENTS

CHICKEN

2 to 2¹/₂ lb/1 to 1.25 kg
meaty chicken pieces (breasts,
thighs and drumsticks)

1 tablespoon cooking oil

¹/₂ cup/2 oz/60 g chopped onion

6 cups/18 oz/510 g firmly packed
shredded cabbage

14¹/₂-oz/525 g can diced
tomatoes

³/₄ cup/4 oz/125 g chopped
green bell pepper (capsicum)

1 to 2 tablespoons packed
brown sugar

1 teaspoon caraway seed

¹/₄ teaspoon salt

¹/₈ teaspoon pepper

1 cup/8 fl oz/250 ml dry
white wine, or apple juice or
apple cider

1 cup/8 fl oz/250 ml chicken
stock

DUMPLINGS

¹/₃ cup/1¹/₂ oz/45 g all-purpose
(plain) flour

¹/₃ cup/2 oz/60 g cornmeal
(polenta)

1 teaspoon baking powder

¹/₄ teaspoon salt

6 tablespoons/3 fl oz/90 ml milk

2 tablespoons cooking oil

2 slices bacon, crisp-cooked
and crumbled

1 tablespoon snipped fresh parsley

Serve individual portions of this hearty European-style recipe in deep earthenware bowls so the dumplings can soak up the savory gravy.

Preparation time 30 minutes
Cooking time 40 to 42 minutes
Makes 6 servings

STEPS AT A GLANCE   Page

For chicken, skin chicken pieces, if desired. Rinse chicken; pat dry. In a 4½-qt/4.5-l Dutch oven or flameproof casserole dish brown chicken in hot oil on all sides over medium heat. Remove from pan. Add onion to pan and cook for 2 to 3 minutes, or until crisp-tender. Add cabbage, undrained tomatoes, green pepper (capsicum), brown sugar, caraway seed, ¼ teaspoon salt and pepper. Stir in wine, apple juice or apple cider. Bring mixture to boiling; return chicken pieces to pan. Reduce heat; cover and simmer for 30 minutes. Stir in chicken stock; return mixture to boiling.

Meanwhile, for dumplings, in a medium mixing bowl stir together the flour, cornmeal (polenta), baking powder and salt. In another bowl combine milk and 2 tablespoons cooking oil; add to dry ingredients and stir with a fork until combined. Stir in bacon and parsley. Drop flour mixture from a tablespoon to make 6 mounds atop the hot, bubbling stew. Cover and simmer for 10 to 12 minutes, or until a toothpick inserted in the center of a dumpling comes out clean. Do not lift cover during cooking. If desired, garnish with additional snipped parsley.

STEPS FOR MAKING DUMPLINGS

STEP 1

Mixing Dumplings

Add milk mixture to flour mixture and stir with a fork just until the dry ingredients are moistened; don't overmix or the dumplings will be tough.

STEP 2

Dropping Dumplings

Scoop up 1 tablespoon of dumpling batter and drop in a mound onto the hot, bubbling liquid. Use a second spoon or rubber spatula to ease the batter off the tablespoon.

STEP 3

Testing for Doneness

To test the dumplings for doneness, insert a toothpick into the thickest part of one; if it comes out clean, the dumplings are ready.

To serve, cover each chicken
leg generously with sauce.
Accompany with pita
bread (a Middle Eastern
flat bread) and sautéed
vegetables.

Chicken with Spicy Yogurt Sauce

Paprika, though often used just for a touch of color, can be quite flavorful.
Using fine-quality paprika, such as the imported Hungarian type,
can make all the difference in the taste of a dish like this.

INGREDIENTS

4 whole chicken legs (drumstick plus thigh), skin removed

1 cup/8 oz/250 g plain low-fat yogurt

2 tablespoons snipped fresh cilantro (fresh coriander/Chinese parsley) or parsley

1 tablespoon curry powder

2 cloves garlic, minced

1 teaspoon ground ginger

1 teaspoon paprika

2 to 3 teaspoons lime juice or lemon juice

1/2 teaspoon salt

2 tablespoons margarine or butter

Fresh cilantro (fresh coriander/Chinese parsley) or parsley (optional)

METHOD FOR MAKING CHICKEN WITH SPICY YOGURT SAUCE

Preparation time 15 minutes
Marinating time 2 to 24 hours
Cooking time 50 to 55 minutes
Makes 4 servings

Rinse chicken; pat dry. Lightly score the flesh of the chicken. Place chicken in a large plastic bag set into a shallow dish. In a small mixing bowl stir together yogurt, cilantro (fresh coriander/Chinese parsley) or parsley, curry powder, garlic, ginger, paprika, lime or lemon juice and salt. Pour yogurt mixture over chicken. Seal bag; turn bag to coat chicken with marinade. Marinate in the refrigerator for 2 to 24 hours, turning bag occasionally.

In a large frying pan melt the margarine or butter over medium heat. Add the chicken legs and the yogurt mixture. Bring to boiling; reduce heat. Cover and simmer for 45 to 50 minutes, or until chicken is tender and no pink remains. Transfer chicken to a serving platter. Boil yogurt mixture gently for about 5 minutes, or until slightly thickened. If desired, garnish with cilantro or parsley.

STEP 1

Scoring Chicken

First remove skin from the chicken legs. Then make shallow parallel marks in the meatiest section of each leg with a chef's knife. These cuts allow the marinade to penetrate the meat.

STEP 2

Marinating Chicken

Combine the marinade ingredients in a small bowl, then transfer to a heavy-duty plastic bag large enough to hold all of the chicken pieces. Add the chicken, seal the bag and turn several times to coat the meat. Lay the bag on its side in a shallow baking dish or bowl.

STEP 3

Turning the Bag

As the chicken marinates, turn the bag several times so that the pieces are immersed in the marinade. This way the juices evenly penetrate all the pieces.

Chicken Mole

The word *mole* comes from a Native American word meaning "concoction" and applies to a variety of blended Mexican sauces that are particularly tasty with chicken and turkey. One of the most famous variations includes a small amount of dark chocolate.

INGREDIENTS

2 to 2¹/₂ lb/1 to 1.25 kg meaty chicken pieces (breasts, thighs and drumsticks), skin removed

2 tablespoons cooking oil

¹/₂ cup/2 oz/60 g chopped onion

2 cloves garlic, minced

10 to 12 fresh or canned tomatillos, chopped

8-oz/250-g can tomato sauce or tomato purée

¹/₃ cup/2 oz/60 g toasted almonds

¹/₄ cup/³/₄ oz/20 g crushed tortilla chips

¹/₄ cup/2 fl oz/60 ml water

2 fresh jalapeño peppers, seeded and chopped, or 2 canned whole green chilies, seeded and chopped

¹/₄ cup/¹/₂ oz/15 g snipped fresh cilantro (fresh coriander/ Chinese parsley)

2 tablespoons toasted sesame seeds

¹/₄ teaspoon ground cinnamon

¹/₄ teaspoon salt

¹/₈ teaspoon ground cloves

1 oz/30 g semi-sweet (plain) chocolate, cut up

Hot cooked rice

Fill individual bowls with seasoned rice, then top with braised chicken pieces and mole. Pass flour tortillas for scooping up the gravy, and lime wedges for garnish.

Preparation time 20 minutes
Cooking time 55 to 60 minutes
Makes 6 servings

Rinse chicken; pat dry. Heat 1 tablespoon of the cooking oil in a 12-in/30-cm heavy frying pan. Add onion and garlic and cook for 3 to 5 minutes, or until onion is tender but not brown. Remove from frying pan and cool slightly.

In a blender container or food processor bowl combine onion mixture, tomatillos, tomato sauce or purée, almonds, tortilla chips, water, jalapeño peppers, cilantro (fresh coriander/Chinese parsley), sesame seeds, cinnamon, salt and cloves. Blend or process until smooth.

Heat remaining oil in frying pan. Add chicken and cook, uncovered, over medium heat for 15 minutes, turning to brown evenly. Add tomato mixture. Bring to boiling; reduce heat. Cover and simmer for 35 to 40 minutes, or until chicken is tender and no pink remains. Transfer chicken to a serving platter; keep warm. Skim off fat from tomato mixture. Add chocolate and cook and stir over low heat until chocolate is melted. Pour over chicken. Serve with rice.

Chicken Filipino-Style

Be sure to use unsweetened coconut milk for this recipe;
it is available at most Asian markets and at many gourmet and specialty food stores.

INGREDIENTS

2 to 2¹/₂ lb/1 to 1.25 kg meaty chicken pieces (breasts, thighs and drumsticks)

2 tablespoons cooking oil

1¹/₂ cups/12 fl oz/375 ml water

¹/₃ cup/2¹/₂ fl oz/80 ml cider vinegar

2 tablespoons soy sauce

3 large cloves garlic, minced

¹/₂ teaspoon whole peppercorns

¹/₂ teaspoon ground black pepper

1 bay leaf

1 medium green bell pepper (capsicum), sliced into thin strips

2 tablespoons cornstarch (cornflour)

2 tablespoons water

1 cup canned unsweetened coconut milk (not cream of coconut)

Hot cooked rice

¹/₄ cup/³/₄ oz/20 g sliced green (spring) onions

Inspired by a classic Filipino recipe, chicken in coconut sauce is served on a mound of steamed white rice and garnished with sliced green onions.

Braising

Preparation time 20 minutes
Cooking time 35 minutes
Makes 6 servings

STEPS AT A GLANCE	Page

If desired, skin chicken. Rinse chicken; pat dry. In a large, heavy frying pan brown chicken in hot oil, turning to brown evenly. Drain off fat. To the pan add water, vinegar, soy sauce, garlic, peppercorns, pepper and bay leaf. Bring to boiling; reduce heat. Cover and simmer for 30 minutes, or until chicken is tender, adding the green bell pepper (capsicum) strips during the last 5 minutes of cooking. Transfer chicken to a serving platter; keep warm.

With a slotted spoon, remove green bell pepper strips and set aside. Stir together cornstarch and 2 tablespoons water; stir into liquid in frying pan. Cook and stir until thickened and bubbly. Cook and stir for 2 minutes more. Stir in coconut milk and the green bell pepper strips. Heat through, but do not boil. Serve chicken and sauce with rice. Sprinkle with green (spring) onions.

Chicken Cassoulet

Cassoulet is a French country dish of much renown.
If desired, substitute two 15-ounce cans Great Northern (cannellini) beans,
drained and rinsed, for the dried beans. Omit cooking the beans and use water
in place of the reserved bean liquid to moisten the cassoulet.

INGREDIENTS

1½ cups/10 oz/300 g dried Great Northern (cannellini) beans

8 cups/64 fl oz/2 l water

¾ cup/2 oz/60 g sliced green (spring) onions

⅓ cup/½ oz/15 g snipped fresh parsley

⅓ cup/2½ fl oz/80 ml dry red or white wine

2 slices bacon, crisp-cooked and crumbled

1 tablespoon tomato paste

3 cloves garlic, minced

½ teaspoon dried thyme, crushed

1 bay leaf

6 chicken drumsticks or thighs (1½ lb/750 g total)

1 tablespoon olive oil or cooking oil

8 oz/250 g fully cooked Polish sausage or other pork sausage, sliced into 1-in/2.5-cm pieces

Serve generous portions of just-baked cassoulet with a mixed green salad and crusty bread for a complete meal.

Preparation time 20 minutes
Soaking time 1 to 24 hours
Cooking time 1½ hours
Baking time 40 to 45 minutes
Makes 4 servings

Rinse dried beans. In a large saucepan or Dutch oven combine beans and 4 cups/32 fl oz/1 l of the water. Bring to boiling; reduce heat and simmer for 2 minutes. Let stand, covered, for 1 hour. (Or, soak beans in 4 cups water overnight.) Drain beans, discarding water. In the same saucepan combine beans and the remaining 4 cups/32 fl oz/1 l of the water. Bring to boiling; reduce heat and simmer for 1½ hours, or until beans are tender. Drain, reserving ⅔ cup/5 fl oz/160 ml of the liquid.

In a large mixing bowl stir together drained beans, reserved bean liquid, green (spring) onion, parsley, wine, bacon, tomato paste, garlic, thyme and bay leaf.

Rinse chicken; pat dry. In a large, heavy frying pan brown the chicken pieces in hot oil, turning to brown evenly. In a Dutch oven or 3-qt/3-l ovenproof casserole layer one third of the beans, all of the chicken and all of the sausage. Cover with remaining bean mixture. Bake, covered, in a preheated 350°F/180°C/Gas Mark 4 oven for 40 to 45 minutes, or until chicken is tender and no pink remains, and beans are heated through.

Chicken with Greek Olives

Use pitted black olives for a mild flavor or briney Kalamata olives
for a more pungent addition to the vinegar-flavored sauce.
Most gourmet markets stock Mediterranean olives in jars or in bulk.

INGREDIENTS

2 to 2½ lb/1 to 1.25 kg meaty chicken pieces (breasts, thighs and drumsticks)

2 tablespoons margarine or butter

4 oz/125 g fresh mushrooms, sliced

2 tablespoons all-purpose (plain) flour

½ teaspoon dried thyme, crushed

¼ teaspoon pepper

1 cup/8 fl oz/250 ml chicken stock

1 tablespoon raspberry vinegar or red wine vinegar

½ cup/2½ oz/75 g Kalamata olives, pitted, or ½ cup/2½ oz/75 g sliced pitted black olives

Hot cooked rice

Arrange several pieces of this tangy chicken on a plate and spoon on the thickened gravy; offer rice pilaf and sautéed peppers and eggplant alongside.

Preparation time 20 minutes
Cooking time 50 to 55 minutes
Makes 4 servings

If desired, skin chicken. Rinse chicken; pat dry. In a large, heavy frying pan cook chicken in margarine or butter over medium heat for about 15 minutes, or until chicken is lightly browned, turning occasionally. Reduce heat; cover and simmer for 30 to 35 minutes, or until chicken is tender and no pink remains. Transfer chicken to a serving platter; keep warm.

Add mushrooms to frying pan and cook over medium heat for 2 to 3 minutes, or until tender. Stir in flour, thyme and pepper. Add chicken stock and raspberry vinegar or red wine vinegar all at once. Cook and stir until thickened and bubbly. Cook and stir for 1 minute more. Add olives and heat through. Pour over chicken. Serve with rice.

Balsamic Vinegar Chicken

Oyster mushrooms, asparagus and pine nuts give crunch and snap
to this delicious, simple braise. Oyster mushrooms are an Asian variety
with pale, creamy flesh and a flowerlike cap.

INGREDIENTS

2 tablespoons olive oil or cooking oil

4 boneless, skinless chicken breast halves (1 lb/500 g total)

1/4 teaspoon white pepper

1/4 cup/3/4 oz/20 g chopped shallots or green (spring) onions

1 cup/8 fl oz/250 ml chicken stock

12 oz/375 g fresh asparagus spears or one 10-oz/315-g package frozen asparagus spears

2 cups/4 oz/125 g fresh oyster mushrooms or other mushrooms

3 tablespoons balsamic vinegar

2 tablespoons margarine or butter, softened

2 tablespoons toasted pine nuts

Hot cooked rice

*Another
time, serve
this easy dish
with orzo pasta
instead of rice.*

Preparation time 20 minutes
Cooking time 20 to 22 minutes
Makes 4 servings

In a large, heavy frying pan heat oil over medium-high heat. Add chicken and cook for 2 minutes. Turn chicken over in pan and sprinkle with white pepper. Add shallots or green (spring) onions to pan; cook for 2 minutes more. Drain off fat. Add chicken stock. Bring to boiling; reduce heat. Cover and simmer for 5 minutes.

Meanwhile, snap off and discard woody bases from fresh asparagus. Cut asparagus into 2-in/5-cm lengths. Halve any large mushrooms. Add asparagus to frying pan; cover and cook for 5 to 7 minutes, or until asparagus is just tender and chicken is tender and no pink remains. Add mushrooms. Cover and cook for 1 minute.

Use a slotted spoon to transfer chicken, asparagus and mushrooms to a serving platter. Keep warm. Add vinegar to liquid in pan. Bring to boiling; boil over high heat for 5 minutes, or until liquid is reduced to ⅓ cup/2½ fl oz/80 ml. Remove pan from heat. Using a wire whisk, blend margarine or butter into liquid in pan. Spoon over chicken; sprinkle with pine nuts. Serve with rice.

Braised Chicken with Apple–Cream Sauce

Since any cut apple surface exposed to air discolors quickly, slice the apples just before cooking them. Rinse the leeks thoroughly before using to remove any dirt that may be hidden between the layers, and slice only the white end.

INGREDIENTS

6 boneless, skinless chicken breast halves (1½ lb/750 g total)

1 tablespoon cooking oil

2 medium cooking apples, cored and sliced

1 medium leek, sliced

½ cup/4 fl oz/125 ml apple juice or apple cider

½ teaspoon instant chicken bouillon (stock) granules

¼ teaspoon dried thyme, crushed

⅛ teaspoon white pepper

⅓ cup/2½ fl oz/80 ml sour cream

2 teaspoons cornstarch (cornflour)

Arrange one chicken breast half on a bed of wild rice and top with sauce, apples and leek. For a cool-weather side dish, try sliced steamed squash.

Preparation time 25 minutes
Cooking time 15 minutes
Makes 6 servings

In a large, heavy frying pan brown the chicken breast halves in hot oil over medium heat, turning once. Remove chicken from pan. Add the apples and leek to the pan and cook over low heat for 2 minutes. Return the chicken breasts to the pan. Add apple juice or cider and chicken bouillon (stock) granules. Sprinkle with thyme and white pepper. Bring to boiling; reduce heat. Cover and simmer for 10 minutes, or until chicken is tender and no pink remains. Remove chicken from pan; keep warm.

In a small mixing bowl stir together sour cream and cornstarch (cornflour). Stir in 2 to 3 tablespoons of the pan juices to thin the mixture; add to remaining pan juices in frying pan. Cook and stir until thickened and bubbly; reduce heat. Cook and stir for 2 minutes more. Spoon sauce over chicken.

Calypso Country Captain

As a result of trade with India during the eighteenth century,
this hearty curried chicken dish became popular in England
and the American colonies, especially in seaports.

INGREDIENTS

8-oz/250-g can pineapple tidbits
(pieces), including juice

4 boneless, skinless chicken breast
halves (1 lb/500 g total)

1/4 cup/1 oz/30 g all-purpose
(plain) flour

1 teaspoon curry powder

1/2 teaspoon salt

1/4 teaspoon pepper

2 tablespoons cooking oil

3/4 cup/4 oz/125 g chopped
green bell pepper (capsicum)

1/2 cup/2 1/2 oz/75 g
chopped onion

2 cloves garlic, minced

14 1/2-oz/455 g can diced
tomatoes

3 tablespoons currants or raisins

1 teaspoon curry powder

1/8 to 1/4 teaspoon crushed
red pepper

1/8 teaspoon salt

1 tablespoon cornstarch

2 to 3 oz/60 to 90 g
coarsely chopped cashew
pieces (optional)

For a complementary side dish, quickly stir-fry cooked white rice with a little onion, a diced peach and toasted almonds.

Preparation time 15 minutes
Cooking time 15 to 20 minutes
Makes 4 servings

STEPS AT A GLANCE   Page
■ Skinning and boning   19–21
■ Braising chicken   228

Drain pineapple, reserving juice. Set aside. Rinse chicken; pat dry. In a plastic bag combine flour, 1 teaspoon curry powder, ¹/₂ teaspoon salt and pepper. Add chicken breasts, one at a time, and shake to coat well.

In a large, heavy frying pan brown the chicken on both sides in hot oil over medium-high heat. Remove chicken from pan. In the oil remaining in the pan, cook green bell pepper (capsicum), onion and garlic until tender but not brown. Stir in drained pineapple, undrained tomatoes, currants, 1 teaspoon curry powder, crushed red pepper and ¹/₈ teaspoon salt. Bring mixture to boiling; return chicken to the pan. Cover and simmer for 8 to 12 minutes, or until chicken is tender and no pink remains. Remove chicken from the pan; keep warm.

Stir together cornstarch and reserved pineapple juice; add to tomato mixture. Cook and stir until thickened and bubbly. Cook and stir for 2 minutes more. Serve sauce over chicken. If desired, garnish with cashews.

About Cashews

Cashew nuts are produced by a tropical tree native to Brazil that grows up to 40 feet/ 12 metres in height. By 1590, the Portuguese had introduced the tree to East Africa and India, from where it spread to India, Sri Lanka and Malaysia. Today the main producers are Brazil, South India and Mozambique. The trees produce fruits, known as cashew apples (but actually pear shaped), inside which the nut develops; when the fruits ripen, the nuts protrude from the end of them in a distinctive and peculiar manner. The shells of the nuts contain an acidic oily substance that can burn and blister the skin, so care must be taken when harvesting them. The oil can be neutralized with wood ash or by heating. Commercially, nuts are roasted in a large kiln then shelled by machine. Once

heated, the nuts are harmless and may be extracted safely from the shells.

The nuts are kidney-shaped and cream-colored. They can be eaten raw, but the flavor intensifies once the nuts are roasted. Cashew nuts are a common ingredient in the cookery of southern India, where they are used whole or ground as a thickening for sauces. They are also added to Chinese and Thai dishes, generally at the end of the cooking time to preserve their flavor and texture. The nuts are commonly served, plain or salted, as a cocktail snack. They are also used in candies and baked products, and are good added to salads and stuffings. Like most nuts, they have a high oil content that makes them prone to rancidity; buy small quantities and store them in a glass jar in the refrigerator.

When serving couscous, fluff it with a fork and top it with chicken, vegetables and beans for a complete meal. A simple green salad is the only additional course needed.

Chicken Couscous

Couscous, though it looks like a whole grain, is a tiny, quick-cooking pasta.
Topped with various meats and vegetables, it is a Moroccan staple.

INGREDIENTS

$^1/_2$ cup/$2^1/_2$ oz/75 g
chopped onion

1 clove garlic, minced

1 tablespoon olive oil or
cooking oil

12 oz/375 g boneless,
skinless chicken thighs, cut
into 1-in/2.5-cm cubes

3 medium carrots, cut into
1-in/2.5-cm pieces

$1^1/_4$ cups/10 fl oz/300 ml
chicken stock

1 cup/4 oz/125 g sliced celery

$^1/_2$ teaspoon salt

$^1/_4$ teaspoon ground cumin

$^1/_4$ teaspoon ground turmeric

$^1/_8$ to $^1/_4$ teaspoon crushed
red (cayenne) pepper

1 medium zucchini (courgette),
cut into $^1/_2 \times ^1/_2 \times$ 1-in/12 mm $\times$
12 mm $\times$ 2.5-cm strips

2 medium tomatoes, peeled,
seeded and chopped

15-oz/470 g can garbanzo beans
(chickpeas), drained

1 cup/5 oz/155 g couscous

METHOD FOR MAKING CHICKEN COUSCOUS

Preparation time 15 minutes
Cooking time 15 to 20 minutes
Makes 4 servings

In a large, heavy frying pan or Dutch oven cook the onion and garlic in hot oil until tender but not brown. Add the chicken, carrots, chicken stock, celery, salt, cumin, turmeric and crushed red pepper. Bring to boiling; reduce heat. Cover and simmer for 20 minutes. Add the zucchini (courgette), tomatoes and garbanzo beans (chickpeas). Cover and cook for 10 minutes more, or until chicken and vegetables are tender.

Meanwhile, prepare couscous according to package directions. To serve, spoon couscous into a serving bowl. Spoon chicken mixture over couscous.

Chicken Rouladen

If you have only enjoyed these rolls prepared with red meat, this version, made with flattened boneless, skinless chicken breasts, will be a pleasant, lighter alternative. Cheese-lovers can add a thin slice of provolone or Swiss over the ham before topping with the roasted red bell pepper.

INGREDIENTS

4 boneless, skinless chicken breast halves (1 lb/500 g total)

4 teaspoons honey mustard or Dijon-style mustard

4 thin slices fully cooked ham (1 1/2 oz/45 g total)

8 oz/250 g canned or bottled roasted red bell peppers (capsicums), drained

1 tablespoon cooking oil

1/2 cup/4 fl oz/125 ml chicken stock

1/2 cup/4 fl oz/125 ml dry white wine

2 tablespoons tomato paste

1 tablespoon snipped fresh basil or 1/2 teaspoon dried basil, crushed

2 teaspoons cornstarch (cornflour)

1 tablespoon water

METHOD FOR MAKING CHICKEN ROULADEN

Preparation time 15 minutes
Cooking time 15 to 20 minutes
Makes 4 servings

Rinse chicken; pat dry. Place each breast half between 2 pieces of plastic wrap. Working from the center to the edges, pound chicken lightly with the flat side of a meat mallet to a 1/4-in/6-mm thickness. Remove plastic wrap.

Spread each of the chicken breast halves with 1 teaspoon of the mustard. Place a slice of ham on each breast, then a roasted red bell pepper half. Fold in long sides of chicken and roll up jelly-roll style. Secure with wooden toothpicks.

In a large, heavy frying pan brown the chicken rolls in hot oil on all sides over medium heat. Add chicken stock and wine. Bring to boiling; reduce heat. Cover and simmer for 25 to 30 minutes, or until chicken is tender and no pink remains. Remove chicken from pan; keep warm.

Stir tomato paste and basil into frying pan. Stir together cornstarch and water; stir into pan. Cook and stir until thickened and bubbly. Cook and stir for 1 to 2 minutes more.

To slice rouladen, remove the chicken rolls to a cutting board and cut into spirals. Arrange the slices decoratively on a plate and drizzle with pan sauce. Egg noodles and steamed vegetables finish the meal.

Spoon the chicken, vegetables and olives from the pan onto a warm platter and ladle the sauce over the chicken mixture.

Chicken Ragoût with Green Olives

**The French word for "stew," *ragoût*, refers to a cooking method
in which the meat is first browned, then cooked slowly in a flavorful liquid.**

INGREDIENTS

3 tablespoons all-purpose (plain) flour

1/2 teaspoon salt

1/4 teaspoon pepper

12 oz/375 g boneless, skinless chicken thighs, cut into 1-in/2.5-cm cubes

3 tablespoons cooking oil

1 large onion, cut into wedges

2 cloves garlic, chopped

2 medium tomatoes, peeled, seeded and chopped, or one 7 1/2-oz/240-g can tomatoes, cut up, including juice

1 tablespoon tomato paste

3/4 cup/6 fl oz/180 ml dry white wine

3/4 cup/6 fl oz/180 ml chicken stock

2 potatoes, peeled and cut into bite-size pieces

1 turnip, peeled and cut into bite-size pieces

1 cup/4 oz/125 g baby carrots or 2 medium carrots, cut into 2-in/5-cm pieces

1/2 teaspoon dried thyme, crushed

1/2 cup/2 1/2 oz/75 g pimiento-stuffed green olives, halved

1 tablespoon snipped fresh parsley

1 tablespoon lemon juice

Preparation time 15 minutes
Cooking time 40 to 45 minutes
Makes 4 servings

Place flour, salt and pepper in a plastic bag. Add chicken cubes a few at a time, shaking bag to coat chicken with flour mixture. In a large, heavy frying pan or Dutch oven brown chicken in hot oil, turning to brown evenly. Remove chicken from pan. Set aside.

Add onion and garlic to oil remaining in pan and cook for 5 minutes. Add the fresh or undrained canned tomatoes and tomato paste; cook 5 minutes more, stirring occasionally. Add browned chicken, wine, chicken stock, potatoes, turnip, carrots and thyme to the pan. Bring to boiling and reduce heat. Cover and simmer for 25 to 30 minutes, or until chicken and vegetables are tender. Add the olives, parsley and lemon juice; heat through.

Chicken Goulash

Serving a dish made with potatoes over noodles is common in Eastern European cuisine. The flavors and textures mesh beautifully. Spaetzle, a tiny German dumpling, is available in most well-stocked supermarkets in the pasta section.

INGREDIENTS

12 oz/375 g boneless, skinless chicken thighs, cut into 1-in/2.5-cm pieces

1/2 cup/4 oz/125 g chopped onion

1 clove garlic, minced

1 to 2 tablespoons cooking oil

2 medium potatoes, peeled and diced

7 1/2-oz/240-g can tomatoes, cut up, including juice

1/4 cup/2 fl oz/60 ml water

1 1/2 teaspoons paprika

1/2 teaspoon salt

1/4 teaspoon caraway seed

1/4 teaspoon dried marjoram, crushed

1/4 teaspoon pepper

Pinch of dried thyme, crushed

2 tablespoons all-purpose (plain) flour

2 tablespoons water

Hot cooked noodles or spaetzle

Sour cream (optional)

Preparation time 25 minutes
Cooking time 17 to 20 minutes
Makes 4 servings

In a large, heavy frying pan cook chicken, onion and garlic in 1 tablespoon hot oil for 3 to 4 minutes, or until chicken is tender and no pink remains. Drain off fat. Add the potatoes, tomatoes, ¼ cup/2 fl oz/60 ml water, paprika, salt, caraway seed, marjoram, pepper and thyme. Bring to boiling; reduce heat. Cover and simmer for 10 to 12 minutes, or until potatoes are tender.

Stir together the flour and 2 tablespoons water; stir into chicken mixture. Cook and stir until thickened and bubbly. Cook and stir for 1 minute more. Serve over hot cooked noodles or spaetzle. If desired, serve with sour cream.

Divide spaetzle or wide egg noodles among large bowls and cover with goulash. Serve a hearty vegetable as an accompaniment.

MICROWAVING
AND POACHING

Microwaving Chicken

No appliance does a better job than the microwave oven for precooking chicken and for saving you time and cleanup. In 20 minutes or less, poultry pieces are ready to use in salads, soups, casseroles and more.

Microwave cooking is extremely easy, but it does differ from conventional methods. If you have never used a microwave oven, some background information will be helpful.

Unlike a regular oven, which uses currents of hot, dry air to cook food, a microwave oven bombards a piece of chicken, for example, with short, high-frequency radio waves. These waves cause the moisture inside the food to vibrate and generate heat. One drawback is that food sometimes cooks unevenly unless it is turned or stirred. Another is that cooking can progress in an instant from juicy to overdone, so most recipes suggest that you check for doneness after the minimum cooking time.

Not all baking dishes are microwave safe. Some manufacturers' labels will tell you, but if you are unsure, try the following test: Fill a glass measuring cup with ½ cup/4 fl oz/125 ml water and place the cup and a baking dish without any metal trim in the microwave. Cook on 100 percent power (high) for 1 minute. If the dish stays cool, go ahead and use it. If it gets hot, use something else.

A final caution: Cooking times for microwave recipes are matched to a specific wattage (in this book, 600 to 700 watts). If the wattage of your oven differs, be sure to adjust the timing, or your food will be underdone or overcooked.

BASIC TOOLS FOR MICROWAVING CHICKEN

Microwave cooking requires a glass, ceramic or plastic dish (never metal), waxed paper to prevent spatters during cooking and tongs to turn the food so that it finishes evenly.

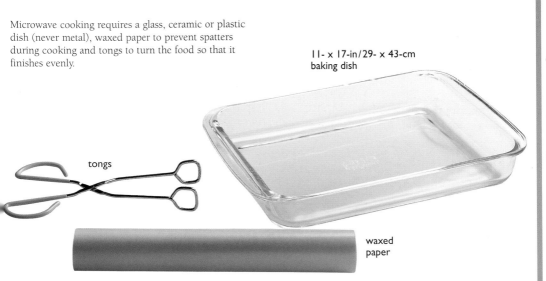

11- x 17-in/29- x 43-cm baking dish

tongs

waxed paper

Basic Microwaved Chicken

Use this basic method whenever you need
sliced or shredded cooked chicken for another recipe,
or even just for a sandwich.

INGREDIENTS

3 lb/1.5 kg meaty chicken pieces
(breasts, thighs and drumsticks)

Preparation time 5 minutes
Cooking time 15 to 20 minutes
Makes about 1½ lb/750 g meat

METHOD FOR MAKING BASIC MICROWAVED CHICKEN

Arrange chicken pieces in a baking dish with meaty portions toward the edges of the dish. Cover with waxed paper.

Microwave on 100 percent power (high) for 15 to 20 minutes, or until chicken is tender and no pink remains, rearranging and turning pieces halfway through cooking time.

Cool for about 15 minutes.

Remove skin and cut or pull meat from the bones. Discard skin and bones. Cut up or shred meat as directed.

The chicken pieces can touch, but shouldn't overlap or they won't cook through.

STEP 1

Arranging Chicken

Use a microwave-safe dish that is large enough to hold the chicken pieces in a single layer. Arrange the chicken, skin-side up (here the breasts have been skinned), with the meatiest parts toward the edges of the dish.

You can also use paper towels cover the food.

STEP 2

Covering Chicken with Waxed Paper

Moist chicken will bubble and spatter as it cooks in the microwave. To keep the juices in the baking dish—not on the oven walls—cover the chicken lightly but completely with a sheet of waxed paper; there is no need to seal the edges.

Rearranging allows the chicken to cook more evenly.

STEP 3

Rearranging Chicken Pieces

Halfway through cooking, pull out the dish with the chicken. With tongs, turn the pieces over and rearrange them so that the less-cooked parts are near the edges of the dish. Cover again with the waxed paper.

Poaching Chicken

Poaching is a very delicate cooking method that bathes poultry in a gently bubbling liquid just below a boil. The result is moist, succulent meat with a light, clean flavor that is ideal for salads, sandwiches and soups. Poached poultry also, as shown in the recipe on page 296, is superb on its own with a light sauce. It is low in fat because no oil is needed, but high in flavor because the poaching liquid draws goodness from the meat and bones.

The key to perfectly poached poultry is to keep the heat at a constant temperature throughout cooking. For the most delicious result, select a pot made of a

material that will heat evenly and maintain temperature and is large enough to allow the hot liquid to move freely around the chicken pieces.

It is best to allow just-cooked poached chicken to sit at room temperature for about 15 minutes. This resting period allows the chicken to cool so you can handle it comfortably and also recirculates the juices so they don't pour out when the meat is cut. If desired, return the bones to the pot after removing the meat and simmer for chicken stock (*see pages 27–29*).

In addition to poaching, the steps on the following pages

demonstrate how to skin, bone, cube and shred precooked chicken, whether poached, microwaved or roasted (*see Basic Roast Chicken, page 36*), to make it ready for the delicious dishes that you'll find in this chapter.

BASIC TOOLS FOR POACHING AND SHREDDING CHICKEN

For poaching, use a large enough pot to hold all of the chicken. Transfer the cooked chicken to a cutting board and slice with a sharp knife or shred with a pair of forks.

heavy saucepan
or cooking pot

cutting board and chef's knife

two forks

Basic Poached Chicken

Tender, moist poached chicken can be a basis for other recipes,
or simply serve it with a sauce and
some steamed vegetables for a quick, easy meal.

INGREDIENTS

3 to 3¹/₂ lb/1.5 to 1.75 kg meaty
chicken pieces (breasts, thighs
and drumsticks) or one whole
3 to 3¹/₂ lb/1.5 to 1.75 broiler-
fryer (roasting) chicken

6 cups/48 fl oz/1.5 l water

Preparation time 5 minutes
Cooking time 40 minutes
Makes about 1¹/₂ lb/750 g meat

METHOD FOR MAKING BASIC POACHED CHICKEN

Place chicken pieces or whole chicken in a 4¹/₂-qt/4.5-l Dutch
oven or heavy cooking pot. Add water. Bring to boiling; reduce heat.
Cover and simmer for 40 minutes, or until chicken is tender and
no pink remains.

Remove chicken from liquid. Let cool for about 15 minutes. Remove
skin and cut or pull meat from the bones. Discard skin and bones.
Cut up or shred meat as directed.

For poaching, bubbles should barely break the surface of the liquid.

STEP 1

Poaching Chicken

Place meaty chicken pieces or a whole chicken in a large Dutch oven. Add water to cover (about 6 cups) and bring to a boil. Reduce heat to low, cover with the lid and simmer until tender and cooked through.

Any bones can be kept for making stock, if desired.

STEP 2

Removing the Skin and Meat

Set the cooled poached chicken on a cutting board. Pull off the skin and discard. The meat should be tender enough that it will release from the bone with a light tug. If not, cut it away with a knife.

Use cooked chicken right away or store, well wrapped, in the refrigerator for a short time until it is needed.

STEP 3

Cutting Up Cooked Chicken

Once the skin is removed and the meat taken off the bone, the cooked chicken can be cut up to suit any recipe. Use a sharp knife and cut it into slices, or cut it into cubes by cutting the slices crosswise.

Pull with the grain of the meat to shred it.

STEP 4

Shredding Cooked Chicken

Some recipes for soups and salads require shredded chicken meat. To shred, steady a piece of cooked, boned, skinned chicken with a fork and pull the fibers apart with a second fork.

About Olives

Small, attractive evergreens with silvery green leaves, olive trees can live—and produce fruit—for hundreds of years. They have flourished throughout their native Mediterranean region since prehistoric times. Olives are mentioned in ancient Greek and Romans writings and in the Bible, and have been cultivated for at least 6,000 years; olive oil was a major export product of Greece as far back as 3,000 BC. Spain is the major producer today, followed by Italy and Greece, but olives will thrive in any Mediterranean-style climate.

There are several varieties; some are best for table olives, others for oil production. Table olives are either green (unripe) or black (ripe). The fruit cannot be eaten straight off the tree; it must first be cured to remove the bitterness, then pickled. Olives are eaten as snacks (sometimes pitted and stuffed with pimientos, almonds or anchovies), or added to salads and meat or chicken dishes.

For oil, only ripe olives are used. The oil is extracted by pressing the olives, traditionally under a large stone, but the modern method is to use a hydraulic press. The oil from the first pressing is called virgin oil. There are several grades, based on their acid content; the least acidic, extra virgin, is the finest and most expensive, with a deliciously fruity odor and flavor. The oil from subsequent pressings, known as pure olive oil, is of a lower grade and must be refined to improve its flavor and keeping qualities. Like most oils, olive oil should always be stored in a cool, dark place.

Parmesan Gougère with Chicken Filling

Traditionally, the baked cream puff pastry known as *gougère*
is made with Gruyère cheese; here we've used Parmesan
and shaped the pastry as a shell for filling.

INGREDIENTS

GOUGÈRE

1 cup/8 fl oz/250 ml water

1/2 cup/4 oz/125 g butter
or margarine

1/8 teaspoon salt

1 cup/4 oz/125 g all-purpose
(plain) flour

4 eggs

1/2 cup/2 oz/60 g finely shredded
fresh Parmesan cheese

2 tablespoons finely shredded
fresh Parmesan cheese

FILLING

2 tablespoons margarine or butter

1 cup/4 oz/125 g thinly sliced
carrots

1 cup/3 oz/90 g fresh
mushrooms, quartered

1 cup/4 oz/125 g sliced zucchini
(courgette)

1/2 cup/2 1/2 oz/75 g chopped
onion

3/4 cup/6 fl oz/180 ml
chicken stock

2 tablespoons all-purpose
(plain) flour

1 teaspoon dried Italian
seasoning, crushed

1/4 teaspoon salt

1/4 teaspoon pepper

2 cups/12 oz/375 g chopped
cooked chicken

1/2 cup/2 oz/60 g shredded
Provolone or mozzarella cheese

1 medium tomato, peeled,
seeded and chopped

Essentially a one-dish meal, this filled gougère needs only a salad accompaniment and an inviting dessert such as fresh fruit and cookies.

Preparation time 15 minutes
Baking time 30 to 40 minutes
Cooking time 10 minutes
Makes 6 servings

For gougère, in a medium saucepan combine water, butter or margarine and salt. Bring to boiling. Add flour all at once, stirring vigorously. Cook and stir until the mixture forms a ball that does not separate. Remove from heat. Cool for 10 minutes. Add eggs, one at a time, beating with a wooden spoon after each addition until smooth. Stir in the 1/2 cup/2 oz/60 g Parmesan cheese. Spread mixture over the bottom and up the sides of a well-greased 10-in/25-cm deep-dish pie plate. Sprinkle with the remaining Parmesan cheese. Bake in a preheated 400°F/200°C/Gas Mark 5 oven for 30 to 40 minutes, or until golden brown.

Meanwhile, for filling, in a large frying pan melt margarine or butter over medium heat. Add the carrots, mushrooms, zucchini (courgette) and onion. Cook and stir for about 5 minutes, or until vegetables are just tender.

Stir together chicken stock, flour, Italian seasoning, salt and pepper. Cook and stir until thickened and bubbly. Cook and stir for 1 minute more. Stir in the cooked chicken, Provolone or mozzarella cheese and tomato. Heat through. Fill hot gougère shell with the hot filling. Serve immediately.

STEPS FOR MAKING GOUGÈRE DOUGH

STEP 1

Stirring Dough

In a medium saucepan, combine water, butter and salt; bring to a boil. Add flour and stir vigorously until dough pulls away from sides of the pan.

STEP 2

Final Stirring

Let the mixture cool before adding the eggs. After the last egg has been added, the dough will lose its lumpiness and be smooth and satiny.

STEP 3

Shaping Gougère

Blend in cheese and spread the dough over the bottom and up the sides of a well-greased pie plate.

Before preparing these salads, let the chicken chill thoroughly. Then arrange lettuce leaves on individual plates to serve as a base and top with a portion of the chicken mixture.

Chicken and Potato Salad with Olive Mayonnaise

If you prefer a milder flavor, use ripe black olives instead of green olives.
The mayonnaise can be made with low-cholesterol liquid egg product (available in
the freezer or refrigerator section of most supermarkets) or with a whole egg.

INGREDIENTS

OLIVE MAYONNAISE

4 oz/125 g pitted green olives, drained

1 egg or 1/4 cup/2 fl oz/60 ml refrigerated or thawed frozen egg product

2 tablespoons lemon juice

1 clove garlic, peeled

1/2 teaspoon dry mustard

1/4 teaspoon salt

1/8 teaspoon ground red (cayenne) pepper

1 cup/8 fl oz/250 ml olive oil or salad oil

SALAD

1 lb/500 g whole tiny new potatoes

2 cups/12 oz/375 g cooked chicken, cut into 3/4-in/2-cm cubes

1/2 cup/1 1/2 oz/45 g finely chopped red bell pepper (capsicum)

1/4 cup/3/4 oz/20 g finely chopped green (spring) onion

Lettuce leaves

Preparation time 25 minutes
Cooking time 10 to 15 minutes
Chilling time 2 hours
Makes 4 servings

For olive mayonnaise, in a food processor bowl or blender container combine olives, egg or egg product, lemon juice, garlic, mustard, salt and ground red (cayenne) pepper. Process or blend until olives are puréed. With the processor or blender running, add oil in a thin, steady stream. (When necessary, stop the machine and use a rubber spatula to clean the sides of the bowl.) Set aside 1 cup/8 fl oz/250 ml of the mayonnaise. Cover and store remaining mayonnaise in the refrigerator for up to 2 weeks.

For salad, cut unpeeled potatoes into quarters. In a medium saucepan cook potatoes, covered, in a small amount of boiling lightly salted water for 10 to 15 minutes or until tender; drain. In a large mixing bowl stir together potatoes, the reserved olive mayonnaise, the cooked chicken, red bell pepper (capsicum), and green (spring) onion. Cover and chill for at least 2 hours. Serve on lettuce leaves.

STEP 1

Puréeing Olives

Combine pitted green olives, egg or egg product,
lemon juice and seasonings in the work bowl of a
food processor or blender. Process until the olives are
chopped to a purée; scrape down the sides of the bowl
with a rubber spatula.

STEP 2

Adding Oil

With the machine running, pour olive oil into the work
bowl in a thin, continuous stream. If necessary, stop the
motor and clean the side of the bowl once again so that
all of the purée is incorporated.

Microwaving and Poaching

Poached Chicken with Star Anise and Ginger

Cut the ginger root into pieces that are large enough to be noticed; the ginger imparts a wonderful flavor that should stand out. While star anise, an ancient Oriental spice, is not a true anise, it adds a similarly intriguing hint of licorice to the sauce.

INGREDIENTS

3 to 3½-lb/1.5 to 1.75 kg whole broiler-fryer (roasting) chicken

2 cups/16 fl oz/500 ml water

¾ cup/6 fl oz/180 ml soy sauce

½ cup/3½ oz/105 g packed brown sugar

3 tablespoons ginger liqueur or dry white wine

1 tablespoon thinly sliced fresh ginger root

2 whole star anise

2 green (spring) onions, cut into thin strips

*Juicy poached
chicken topped
with a subtle sauce
is delicious with
noodles and stir-fried
Asian-style vegetables.*

METHOD FOR MAKING POACHED CHICKEN WITH STAR ANISE AND GINGER

Preparation time 15 minutes
Cooking time 55 to 60 minutes
Makes 6 servings

STEPS AT A GLANCE   Page
■ Poaching chicken   285–286

Rinse chicken; pat dry. In a Dutch oven or heavy cooking pot combine water, soy sauce, brown sugar, ginger liqueur or wine, ginger root and star anise. Place the chicken, breast-side down, in the Dutch oven. Bring to boiling; reduce heat. Cover and simmer for 25 minutes. Turn chicken over and simmer, covered, for 25 to 30 minutes more, or until chicken is tender and no pink remains, basting frequently during the last 10 minutes. Remove chicken from pan; keep warm.

Skim fat from cooking liquid. Strain liquid through several layers of 100 percent cotton cheesecloth or muslin; discard ginger and anise. Reserve 1½ cups/12 fl oz/375 ml of the liquid; discard remaining liquid. Return the reserved liquid to the Dutch oven. Boil, uncovered, for 3 to 4 minutes, or until reduced to ½ cup/4 fl oz/125 ml.

To serve, cut the chicken into serving-sized pieces. Spoon some of the reduced liquid over each serving and pass the remainder. Garnish with the green (spring) onion strips.

Island Chicken Sandwiches

For optimum flavor, use freshly grated lime peel and fresh lime juice.
You will be able to extract more juice if the lime is at room temperature and you roll it
back and forth under your palm a few times before squeezing it. Be sure to wear gloves
when handling fresh chilies to protect your eyes and skin against burning.

INGREDIENTS

3 to 3¹/₂-lb/1.5 to 1.75 kg whole broiler-fryer (roasting) chicken, cut up

6 cups/48 fl oz/1.5 l water

1 teaspoon finely shredded lime peel

¹/₄ cup/2 fl oz/60 ml fresh lime juice

¹/₂ teaspoon salt

¹/₄ teaspoon lemon pepper

¹/₄ cup/³/₄ oz/20 g flaked coconut

¹/₂ cup/1¹/₂ oz/45 g finely chopped green (spring) onion

2 jalapeño peppers or small hot chilies, finely chopped

Pita bread rounds or flour tortillas

Spinach leaves and/or peeled and sliced papaya or mango

Stuff this tropical chicken salad into pita bread, or roll in a tortilla, for a light lunch.

Preparation time 25 minutes
Cooking time 40 minutes
Makes 4 to 6 servings

Rinse chicken; pat dry. Place chicken in a 4½-qt/4.5 l Dutch oven or heavy cooking pot. Add water. Bring to boiling; reduce heat. Simmer, covered, for 40 minutes, or until chicken is tender and no pink remains. Remove chicken from Dutch oven; reserve the stock for another use. When cool enough to handle, skin, bone and shred chicken.

In a large mixing bowl combine warm chicken, lime peel, lime juice, salt and lemon pepper; toss to mix. Stir in coconut, green onion and jalapeño peppers or small hot chilies.

Line pita pockets or tortillas with spinach and/or papaya or mango and add chicken mixture; roll up the flour tortillas, if using.

Microwaving and Poaching

Taipei Chicken with Mixed Greens

You could add about ½ cup/4 fl oz/125 ml of wine or dry sherry
to the poaching liquid or to the microwave dish when cooking the chicken
to add flavor and help keep the meat moist.

INGREDIENTS

2 cups/12 oz/375 g shredded
cooked chicken, warmed

1 cup/3 oz/90 g packaged crisp
chow mein noodles

¼ cup/¾ oz/20 g thinly sliced
green (spring) onions

¼ cup/2 fl oz/60 ml soy sauce

2 tablespoons toasted sesame oil

2 tablespoons rice vinegar

2 tablespoons water

2 teaspoons sugar

2 teaspoons grated fresh ginger
root

1 small red or green jalapeño
pepper or hot chili, seeded
and finely chopped

4 cups/12 oz/375 g mixed
fresh salad greens

For a light meal, toss warm shredded chicken with a hot soy-sesame sauce. Arrange a layer of fresh greens on individual plates and cover with a portion of the chicken.

303

METHOD FOR MAKING TAIPEI CHICKEN WITH MIXED GREENS

Preparation time 20 minutes
Cooking time 3 to 5 minutes
Makes 4 servings

In a large mixing bowl combine the chicken, chow mein noodles and green (spring) onion.

In a small saucepan stir together soy sauce, sesame oil, vinegar, water, sugar, ginger root and jalapeño pepper or chili. Bring to boiling, stirring to dissolve the sugar. Remove from heat and pour over the chicken mixture. Toss to mix. Serve atop mixed salad greens.

Curried Chicken Salad

Try other fruits in this salad, such as apples,
red or green seedless grapes or pineapple. Two tablespoons of
golden raisins or dried currants may also be added.

INGREDIENTS

2 tablespoons chutney

1/2 cup/4 fl oz/125 ml
mayonnaise or salad dressing

1/2 teaspoon curry powder

1/2 cup/3 oz/90 g lightly salted
whole almonds

2 cups/12 oz/375 g chopped
cooked chicken

2 red or green unpeeled pears,
cored and coarsely chopped

Spinach leaves

Preparation time 15 minutes
Chilling time 2 to 24 hours
Makes 4 to 6 servings

Snip or chop any large pieces of fruit in the chutney. In a small mixing bowl stir together chutney, mayonnaise or salad dressing and curry powder.

Coarsely chop 1/3 cup/2 oz/60 g of the almonds. In a large mixing bowl combine chicken, pears and chopped almonds. Add mayonnaise mixture and mix well. Cover and chill for 2 to 24 hours. Serve on spinach-lined plates. Garnish with remaining whole almonds.

Add a touch of heat to this cool salad by adding spicy chutney to the dressing.

Glossary

**Here you'll find information on selecting, purchasing
and storing ingredients used in this book.**

chili

BASIL

An intensely aromatic green-leafed herb, basil has a sweet-to-peppery
licorice-like flavor that enhances tomato-based dishes and sauces, and Italian
pesto. Fresh basil is plentiful in summer; dried basil is always available in supermarket spice sections.
Immerse freshly cut stems in 2 in/5 cm of water, cover with a plastic bag and refrigerate for several days.

BAY LEAF

Pungent, woodsy bay leaves, from the evergreen bay tree, add a distinctive flavor to soups, stews and
marinades, and are an essential part of a *bouquet garni*. Add whole leaves during cooking, then remove
before serving. Dried bay leaves are on all supermarket spice shelves; store in an airtight container in a
cool, dark spot and use within a year.

BELL PEPPERS (CAPSICUMS)

Bell peppers are mildly flavored, with a crisp, crunchy texture. Green ones are most common, but red,
orange, yellow and purple peppers are also available. Bell peppers are an excellent source of vitamin C.
Some varieties are dried and ground to make paprika. Choose firm, shiny, unbruised peppers; avoid those
with wet stems. Store for up to 5 days in the refrigerator.

CHILIES

There are many varieties of chilies, both hot and mild. They are sold fresh or canned and pickled. Finely ground red pepper and red pepper flakes, both hot and pungent blends of dried red chilies, are sold as spices. Hot peppers contain oils that burn eyes and skin, so always wear rubber gloves or protect your hands with plastic bags when cutting up any fresh chili.

COCONUT MILK

A staple ingredient in Thai curries and used in beverages, sauces, soups and desserts throughout southeast Asia, unsweetened coconut milk is made from water and coconut pulp. Rich and creamy, it is available in cans at specialty food stores. Do not substitute cream of coconut.

EGGPLANT (AUBERGINE)

This versatile vegetable is available in several forms, primarily the large, pear-shaped Western or Italian type and the slender Asian varieties. Most are purple-skinned, although some are white. When cooked, all eggplants have a mild flavor and tender, creamy flesh. Look for plump, glossy, heavy eggplants with taut skin and no bruises or scratches. Refrigerate in a plastic bag for up to 2 days.

FENNEL

A creamy-white to pale-green vegetable with a broad, bulbous base, tubular stalks and feathery leaves, fennel has a celery-like texture and faintly licorice flavor that becomes more delicate when cooked. Select bulbs that are free of cracks or brown spots. Refrigerate in a plastic bag for up to 4 days.

fennel

GINGER

Spicy-sweet fresh ginger root, actually the rhizome of a semi-tropical plant, is a common seasoning in many Asian cuisines. The papery skin is generally removed before use. Pieces of ginger preserved in syrup, usually labeled "stem ginger in syrup", are popular in sweet dishes. Select fresh ginger roots that are firm, not shriveled. Wrap in a paper towel and refrigerate for 2 to 3 weeks. Store ground and crystallized ginger for up to 6 months.

HOT BEAN PASTE

Made from a fermented soybean sauce and crushed hot chilies, this Asian cooking condiment thickens and wakes up all kinds of foods. Look for it in jars or cans in specialty markets or in the Asian food section of well-stocked supermarkets. Stays fresh indefinitely in the refrigerator.

LEEK

mushrooms

A mildly flavored member of the onion family. Firm, small-to-medium leeks with crisp green leaves are the best choice; large ones tend to be tough. Refrigerate in a plastic bag for up to 5 days. Before using, rinse leeks carefully, as dirt tends to get trapped between the layers.

MUSHROOMS

A fungus, mushrooms are available in numerous varieties, colors and sizes. Select firm, fresh, plump mushrooms that aren't slimy or bruised. Store in the refrigerator, lightly wrapped in paper towels or in a paper bag, never in plastic, which will make them sweat and perish. Use right away.

saffron

Glossary

OLIVES

The fruit of the silvery-leafed olive tree, olives are either cured for eating or pressed for their oil. There are dozens of varieties, both green and black. The former are underripe, with a salty, tart flavor; they are packed pitted or unpitted in jars or cans. Pitted green olives are sometimes stuffed with red pimiento, tiny onions or whole blanched almonds. Black olives, including Kalamatas and Niçoises, are ripe, with a smooth, mellow flavor. Buy them in cans, jars or in bulk.

PAPRIKA

Ground from dried, mild bell peppers (capsicums), paprika adds a dash of red to dressings, stews, egg and rice dishes and sausages. Imported sweet or hot Hungarian paprika is more pungent than the mild Spanish type. There is also a smoked type that inparts a rich, smoky aroma and flavor. Most supermarkets stock paprika in their spice section. Store in a cool, dry spot.

PARSLEY

This widely used, bright-green herb adds a clean, fresh flavor and decorative color to almost any dish. Curly-leaf parsley is ruffled, with a slightly peppery taste; Italian parsley is flat-leafed and more pungent. Chinese parsley, also known as cilantro, is actually the leaves of the coriander plant. Select healthy-looking bunches that aren't wilted or brown. To store, rinse and shake off excess moisture. Wrap in paper towels, then in a plastic bag, and refrigerate for up to 1 week.

bell peppers

SAFFRON

At least 225,000 stigmas from a special variety of crocus are needed to make just 1 lb/500 g of yellow-orange saffron, the world's costliest spice. Luckily, most dishes only require a small amount. To extract the maximum flavor and color, saffron threads or powder should be steeped in hot liquid before being added to the recipe. The threads stay pungent longer than the powder; both are available where spices are sold. Saffron threads are preferable to the ground form, which can easily be adulterated with cheaper spices or with dyes. Saffron quickly loses its pungency, so buy it in small quantities and use it as soon as possible.

SAGE

Gray-green sage is a fragrant perennial herb, native to southern Europe, that has a slightly bitter flavor and distinctive aroma. It is widely used with poultry and is a staple seasoning for sausages. Wash the leaves and shake off excess water; wrap in paper towels and refrigerate in a plastic bag for up to 1 week. Dried sage is stocked with other seasonings in all supermarkets. Bottled dry leaves will keep for up to 2 years and ground sage for up to 6 months.

SESAME OIL

There are various types of sesame oil. Those made from untoasted seeds are pale and have a mild flavor; those from toasted seeds are amber-colored and have a pronounced, nutty flavor. The latter is used in Asia, though less for cooking than as a seasoning. Most well-stocked supermarkets and Asian markets carry sesame oil.

SHALLOTS

This diminutive member of the onion family is formed in the same way as garlic, with a head made up of more than one clove. Shallots have a milder flavor than most onions and need only quick cooking. Look for firm, well-shaped heads that are not sprouting. Store in a cool, dry place for up to 1 month.

THYME

Spicy and pungent, thyme is rarely used alone. More often, it is blended with other herbs to give complexity to poultry, veal and other dishes. It is sold fresh and dried. Store fresh thyme wrapped in paper towels in a plastic bag; refrigerate for 1 week. Store dried thyme for up to 2 years.

TOMATILLOS

Despite their similar name, tomatillos are not tomatoes but rather small, green ground cherries with a papery brown husk. Their tart, lemony flavor adds a bite to Mexican sauces and stews. They are available fresh and canned at Latin American markets and well-stocked supermarkets. Choose fresh, firm tomatillos with tight-fitting husks; refrigerate in a paper bag for up to 10 days.

tomatillos

VINEGAR

Expose alcohol to a particular strain of airborne bacteria and it becomes vinegar. This acidic liquid enlivens salad dressings, marinades and sauces, as well as vegetables and noodles. There are many varieties, from fine, mellow salad vinegars, such as balsamic vinegar, to coarser types used for pickling. Vinegar lasts indefinitely, but it is best to store it away from light and heat.

Index

Entries in *italics* indicate illustrations and photos.

ACKNOWLEDGMENTS

Weldon Owen would like to thank the following people: Sarah Anderson, Lisa Boehm, Trudie Craig, Peta Gorman, Michael Hann, Puddingburn Publishing Services (index)

Photography Ad-Libitum/Stuart Bowey, Kevin Candland, Rowan Fotheringham, Chris Shorten

Styling Peggy Fallon, Laura Ferguson, Heidi Gintner, Merilee Hague, Jane Hann, Susan Massey, Vicki Roberts-Russell